COAST

A CELEBRATION OF BRITAIN'S COASTAL HERITAGE

THE CLIFFS OF GAMMON HEAD AND PRAWLE POINT,
NEAR SALCOMBE, DEVON

CHRISTOPHER SOMERVILLE

COAST

A CELEBRATION OF BRITAIN'S COASTAL HERITAGE

THE ISLE OF BUTE, SCOTLAND

DOWNHILL BEACH, NORTHERN IRELAND

Gazetteer 128

Foreword

One night during the filming of *Coast* for BBC 2,
I found myself on a fishing boat pitching about on
the swell several miles off the coast of Cornwall.
It was winter, and the deck was awash with seawater.
To the north, the sepulchral cliffs of Land's End were
bathed in starlight. After tensely stalking a shoal of
sardines for what seemed an eternity, the skipper
shot the net, the boat circled, and the two crewmen
winched from the sea thousands of silvery fish.

That night captured the beauty and the bounty of
the UK's coast. And it illuminated the tenacity of
the people who choose to wrest a living from this
challenging water-margin. It's always been a restless
place, but with warming oceans and rising sea levels,
the species who colonize these shores – both human
and marine – are set to witness dramatic changes of
habitat over the coming century.

As islanders we are drawn to the edge; it is where
we sense most strongly the essence of our floating
landmass. Christopher Somerville's elegant book
is both an evocation of our most precious asset and
a call to enjoy and protect it.

NICHOLAS CRANE
Lead Presenter on *Coast*

CALDEY ISLAND, DYFED, WALES

Introduction

The coastlines of Great Britain and Northern Ireland are famed for their beauty and diversity – and no wonder. These islands possess the most varied and dramatic coast of any country of comparable size in the world.

Hearing the ecstatic cries of children running in and out of the sea on a sunny Pembrokeshire morning, you lie back dreamily on the sands as if cradled by the green arms of the headlands. A howling gale in the Shetland Islands, tossing the fishing boats like toys and making the cliffs shudder as storm waves thump into black granite, offers the other side of the coin. Then, on a windy sea wall by a lonely Essex creek, watching a skein of brent geese hurry across a green and pink winter sunset, you sense the moody spirit of a coast of marshes and mud flats, ruled by tides and roofed in by vast skies.

Coast opens new windows on a rich heritage in a region-by-region celebration of this extraordinary landscape, its wild history and the salty characters whose stories are bound up with it. And the extensive Gazetteer section provides a practical key to getting out there and enjoying this great British and Northern Irish coastline in all its power and glory.

CHRISTOPHER SOMERVILLE

The Defiant Coast
THE STRAITS OF DOVER TO THE EXE ESTUARY

It's 21 miles from Calais to Dover breakwater. Viewed from the French shore, the White Cliffs of Dover form a solid wall of white that looks almost close enough to touch. From the cliffs of Cap Gris-Nez, with a decent telescope, you can make out the colour of the fishermen's oilskins in Dover Harbour. A Napoleonic invasion barge with a sail and a couple of hundred lusty soldiers to take turns at the oars could have crossed the Straits of Dover under the cover of a short summer's night. A fast torpedo boat could do it in less than half an hour, a Junkers 88 bomber in five minutes. And a shell fired from a Second World War railway gun or heavy battery on the French cliffs would be plunging down on Dover in a matter of seconds.

It's no wonder that the 125-mile seaboard from Dover round to the Royal Navy's home base of Portsmouth is the most heavily fortified stretch of coastline in Britain. Since the Normans came ashore on the

PORTSMOUTH HAS ITS WONDERFUL HISTORIC DOCKYARD, BUT IT IS ALSO A WORKING ROYAL NAVY BASE – HERE TYPE 42 DESTROYER HMS *CARDIFF* AND TYPE 23 FRIGATES *GRAFTON* AND *MARLBOROUGH* LIE ALONGSIDE.

1 ■ THE DEFIANT COAST
Dover – Dungeness – Eastbourne – Portsmouth – Brighton – Bournemouth – Poole – Lyme Regis – Weymouth – Exeter

coast of East Sussex in 1066 and beat the English at the Battle of
Hastings, invasion plans have been laid by many and various
would-be conquerors of this island. The sea crossing of the Straits
of Dover seems so short, such an insignificant little jump for an army
to take. Yet somehow, by a mixture of belligerent defiance, alertness
and extraordinary good luck, the British have remained uninvaded
throughout those 1000 years. Vigilance has had to be the watchword,
all along the shore of chalk cliffs, pebble beaches and marshes that so
closely face Continental Europe. The cost of remaining free has been
paid in forts, gun batteries, castles and lookout posts. The coasts of
Kent, Sussex and Hampshire fairly bristle with fortifications and early
warning systems, with weather-beaten fortlets in the sea and slit-eyed
towers, bunkers and blockhouses along the shore, from the iconic
White Cliffs to the narrow waterway that leads from Portsmouth
Harbour into the open sea.

THE WHITE CLIFFS BETWEEN EAST DEAN AND SEAFORD,
EAST SUSSEX, COMPOSED OF CHALK HUNDREDS OF FEET THICK,
STAND BARED LIKE TEETH AT ALL-COMERS ACROSS THE ENGLISH
CHANNEL – THE SYMBOL OF THIS ISLAND NATION'S DEFIANT
COAST.

King Henry VIII ordered the first great wave
of castle-building after his split with the
Church of Rome brought fears of an invasion
by France and Spain, the great Catholic
powers of Europe. Magnificent examples
of the King's Kentish coast forts, their walls
strengthened with bastions, still stand at
Dover, Deal and Walmer; while Hurst Castle,
near Lymington in Hampshire, dramatically
sited out in the Solent at the tip of its shingle
spit, is another superb Tudor stronghold.

But it was the nineteenth century that saw
the biggest expansion of coast fortifications.
In response to the very real threat of invasion
by Napoleon Bonaparte's forces, from 1805
to 1810 a string of 74 Martello towers was
built between Folkestone in Kent and Seaford
in Sussex. Twenty-five still stand, some of
them now converted into museums, such
as those at Eastbourne, Seaford and
Dymchurch. The military object of these
stark, squat little turrets with their tiny
windows was to fire on any invading force
in any direction with the cannon mounted
on their roofs. Their real value, however,
was as highly visible deterrents, and as
morale-boosters for the British public.

WALMER CASTLE WAS BUILT FROM 1539 TO 1540 BY
KING HENRY VIII TO COUNTER THE THREAT OF FRENCH
INVASION. ITS QUATREFOIL SHAPE AND RELATIVELY LOW
WALLS GAVE IT STRENGTH AND A WIDE FIELD OF FIRE,
WHILE REDUCING ITS SIZE AS A TARGET.

1 ■ THE DEFIANT COAST
Dover – Dungeness – Eastbourne – Portsmouth – Brighton –
Bournemouth – Poole – Lyme Regis – Weymouth – Exeter

BUILT IN THE MID-SOLENT FROM 1867 TO 1868 TO GUARD AGAINST FRENCH INVASION, THE STURDY BASTION OF SPITBANK FORT IS A GREAT EXAMPLE OF A 'PALMERSTON'S FOLLY'.

Later in the century an invasion scare centred around Bonaparte's great-nephew, Emperor Napoleon III. Under Prime Minister Lord Henry Palmerston, a vast programme of fort-building took place in the 1860s and 1870s, and these massive stone and concrete 'Palmerston's Follies' can be seen in many places along the stretches of coast that face the Continent. They range from giant circular gun emplacements founded on shoal banks out at sea, such as Spitbank Fort guarding Portsmouth, to great complexes of bunkers,

barracks, breakwaters and batteries, such as the fortifications guarding Portland Harbour in Dorset and the enormous Fort Brockhurst and Fort Nelson that shielded Portsmouth from attack.

So to the wars of the twentieth century. The Hellfire Corner tunnels dug into the White Cliffs of Dover during Napoleonic times were enlarged during the Second World War and used as a base for the Dunkirk evacuation operation, and employed again during the

POOLE HARBOUR IS ONE OF BRITAIN'S FINEST AND LARGEST NATURAL HARBOURS. IN THE MIDDLE LIES THE NATIONAL TRUST NATURE RESERVE OF BROWNSEA ISLAND, ONE OF THE LAST REFUGES IN SOUTHERN ENGLAND FOR THE RED SQUIRREL.

Cold War as a nuclear command centre. At Dungeness you can see the concrete 'sound mirrors' that were designed to indicate approaching enemy aircraft engines in the days before radar. Another grim reminder of Hitler's era is what little remains of the SS concentration camp known as Sylt, operated between March 1943 and June 1944 on Alderney, one of the Channel Islands occupied by the Germans.

International wars were not the only conflicts to bedevil this coast. Its proximity to the Continent (the Kent and Sussex seaboard in particular), as well as punitive import taxes, meant that during the eighteenth and early nineteenth centuries smuggling was rife. Local gangs and the excise men were at loggerheads, often with bloody consequences. The Hawkhurst gang of West Kent, the Alfriston gang of East Sussex and the Findon gang of West Sussex were notorious, and dozens of other local gangs are still remembered and talked about today.

Britain's south-east coastline comprises two distinct halves. Once you venture beyond Southampton into Dorset, the theme of human conflict starts to give way to the gentler influence of nature. The great bay of Poole Harbour with its broad saltmarshes and tidal muds is a wonderful larder for

THE MEDIEVAL SWANNERY AT ABBOTSBURY IS HOME TO HUNDREDS OF MUTE SWANS – NO LONGER BRED FOR THE TABLE OF THE ABBOT AND HIS GUESTS, BUT FREE TO ROAM AND FORAGE IN THE PROTECTED WATERS OF THE FLEET.

1 ■ THE DEFIANT COAST
Dover – Dungeness – Eastbourne – Portsmouth – Brighton –
Bournemouth – Poole – Lyme Regis – Weymouth – Exeter

wading birds, while the brackish Fleet Lagoon
behind Chesil Beach's immense shingle bank
is another fine site for birds, including the
swans of Abbotsbury Swannery.

But it is the remarkable geological foundations
that have earned this stretch of coast its rating
as a UNESCO World Heritage Site. Exposed
here in superb detail is a 185-million-year-old
rock sandwich: red sandstone underpinning
limestone and a band of slippery black gault
clay, with greensand and chalk topping it off.
The various layers of rock – originally stacked
horizontally, the oldest at the bottom, the
youngest on top – were tilted to the east by
ancient subterranean upheavals. The oldest
rock, near Exeter in the west, is dusky red
sandstone laid down in the Triassic period
when southern England was one huge sun-
baked desert. Most of the Jurassic-era material
– dark clay and pale limestone, deposited
between 200 and 140 million years ago in a
warm sea that flooded the old red desert –
lies towards the middle of the coast. And the
young Cretaceous chalk, created from the
bodies of countless minuscule forms of marine
life settling on the bed of a clear, shallow sea,
is seen mostly in the east of the region.

RED, WHITE AND BROWN STRATA OF SANDSTONE, LIMESTONE
AND CLAY STRIPE THE CLIFFS OF THE 'JURASSIC COAST' OF
DORSET AND EAST DEVON, SO GEOLOGICALLY RICH THAT IT HAS
BEEN DESIGNATED A UNESCO WORLD HERITAGE SITE.

THE FOSSIL-BEARING LIAS CLAYS ARE ESPECIALLY PRODUCTIVE AND EASY TO ACCESS ON THE BEACHES AROUND LYME REGIS. HEREABOUTS THEY LITTER THE SHORE, HAVING FALLEN FROM THE UNSTABLE CLIFFS OF THIS AREA OF WEST DORSET.

Everything is shaky, unstable and liable to slip and tumble; hence the odd shapes of the cliffs, their multicoloured pointed heads; their crazily tilted strata; their caves, arches and ledges. It's a geology that causes frequent landslips, which have made this coast the prime fossil-hunting region of Britain, especially around Lyme Regis in west Dorset. The town's favourite daughter is Mary Anning (1799–1847), an expert in recovering fossils of great marine reptiles. Thanks to her discoveries and those of many others, the Dorset and East Devon coast has become known as the 'Jurassic Coast', a brilliant place to hunt for fossils, whether you are a learned palaeontologist or a casual stroller in this beautiful part of the world.

THE PETRIFIED TREE STUMPS OF A PREHISTORIC FOREST FORM THESE
CURIOUS BULGY CRATERS IN THE ROCKS AROUND LULWORTH COVE,
ONE OF THE JEWELS OF THE 'JURASSIC COAST'.

The Wild West

THE EXE ESTUARY TO THE SEVERN ESTUARY

A summer visitor to Devon, travelling in a railway carriage along the coast of the English Riviera and looking out over the neat villas and promenades of Paignton and Torquay to the mild waters of Tor Bay, could easily get the impression that the West Country's long peninsula is all about happy holidays and sunny weather. So it is – up to a point. Britain's south-western corner, blessed with a warm sea and a mild climate, has been the country's natural summertime playground for the best part of 200 years, ever since the railways brought the holidaymakers through Somerset and Devon into Cornwall. But that's only half the story out here in the Wild West, where the toe-tip of the British Isles pokes out into the Atlantic Ocean.

Traditional bucket-and-spade holidays with sandy beaches and a safe, clean sea have been the staple of the West Country's seaside trade since those railway tourists first arrived in early Victorian times. But today's surfers, riding the crashing rollers at Polzeath in Cornwall or up at Croyde on Devon's north coast, could tell you how wild the sea can become and how much of a punch it packs, even in good weather. When the Atlantic becomes properly roused in a January gale, the sea throws fishing boats around like toys and sends big ships scurrying into port. Breakwaters, harbour walls and even the cliffs of granite and sandstone shudder as waves burst against them. Rough weather reveals the power of wind, sea and salt spray to scour this harsh western landscape and reduce life to a bare struggle for survival.

TORQUAY IS A GOOD EXAMPLE OF A SUCCESSFUL VICTORIAN SEASIDE RESORT FOUNDED ON A FISHING HARBOUR, WITH BEAUTIFUL VIEWS, PLENTY OF SANDY BEACHES AND GOOD RAILWAY CONNECTIONS WITH THE REST OF THE COUNTRY.

EVEN IN CALM WEATHER, THE CONSTRICTED HARBOUR OF POLZEATH PRODUCES WELL-SPACED WAVES; IN THE TEETH OF A GOOD ATLANTIC BLOW IT BECOMES ONE OF THE UK'S BEST SURFING BEACHES.

SPEED, HEIGHT, SPRAY, ATHLETICISM AND THE DRAMA OF A SMALL FIGURE FLYING FROM THE BACK
OF A BIG WAVE – THE MAGIC OF RIDING THE BOARD IS WELL CAUGHT IN THIS SHOT OF A SURFER AT
CROYDE BAY, NORTH DEVON.

The land itself seems to change form and mood between the holiday season and the back end of the year. The Cornish clifftops that are bright with sea pinks and harebells all summer take on colours of dun and ochre, hinting at the strength and dourness of the granite beneath. The red sandstone cliffs of Devon hide their fiery glow under a coat of dull crimson, while the mud flats of the Somerset coast glint dully under wintry skies. This is the time when the underlying hardness of the peninsula is exposed and a stranger can appreciate how tough it has always been to scratch your living as a farmer or a fisherman along these weather-beaten coasts. Salt, wind and rain make dairy farming a trial and every harvest a gamble. The trawlers that work out of ports such as Newlyn and Brixham are sturdy vessels crewed by determined men, but wild weather can keep them stormbound for days on end. As for a window into the harshness of the tin miner's lot in earlier days – the industry reached its zenith in the nineteenth century – one only has to glance at the bleak ruins of the engine houses and tall industrial chimneys in their windswept locations all along the northern coastline of west Cornwall to imagine the harsh, unrelenting struggle of life back then.

TRAWLERS LARGE AND SMALL TIE UP ALONGSIDE THE GREAT BREAKWATERS AT NEWLYN. THESE MIGHTY BARRIERS SHELTER CORNWALL'S PREMIER FISHING FLEET AGAINST THE ATLANTIC WEATHER.

THE DEVON PORT OF BRIXHAM WAS FAMOUS FOR ITS CLINKER-BUILT, GAFF-RIGGED SAILING TRAWLERS – THERE WERE SAID TO BE SO MANY IN THE TOWN'S NINETEENTH-CENTURY HEYDAY THAT A FISHERMAN COULD WALK DRYSHOD ACROSS THEIR DECKS FROM ONE SIDE OF THE HARBOUR TO THE OTHER.

It is not only the weather that is wild down in the south-west. The waters off Devon, Cornwall and Somerset are some of the trickiest and most treacherous around the British Isles. In the days of sail, when ships were at the mercy of the wind, lives were lost by shipwreck with heartbreaking frequency. Down the centuries, hundreds of vessels were wrecked, with thousands of people drowned, on the Skerries shingle bank that lies just under the surface of Start Bay, the great scoop of cliffs and sands where the south-trending coast of South Devon turns to run west towards Cornwall.

The Cornish coast is indented with scores of lee-shore traps in the form of coves, and seeded with sly rocks, reefs and shoals. The Somerset shore, from the wide Bristol Channel up into the narrowing throat of the Severn Estuary, is a maze of channels, rock scars and sandbanks that only an expert pilot can negotiate on an ebb tide. These dangers have much diminished since the invention of radar and sophisticated navigation equipment, but they still lurk for the unwary or unlucky. Fortunately for seafarers in trouble, the West Country lifeboat crews, though no longer made up exclusively of local fishermen, are as brave and resourceful as ever they were. Sometimes they pay for their courage with their lives,

as happened just before Christmas 1981, when all eight crewmen of the Penlee lifeboat *Solomon Browne* lost their lives going to the assistance of the bulk carrier *Union Star* in hurricane-force winds and mountainous seas.

Wild places can breed wild people, and the West Country coast has produced some of the wildest. More remote in the eighteenth and nineteenth centuries, the area was a smuggler's heaven. The excisemen had an almost impossible job curbing the likes of the 'King of Prussia' (John Carter of Prussia Cove near Porthleven, West Cornwall) and the 'Rob Roy of the West' (Jack Rattenbury of Beer in East Devon), and their job was made no easier by landowners such as Sir William Wyndham of Watchet and Colonel Luttrell of Dunster, both of West Somerset, who were prepared to turn a blind eye to the activities of their local 'free traders'. Smuggling was a bit of a game, although one that could turn violent at any time; but wrecking was another matter altogether.

WINTER WEATHER CAN BE FEROCIOUS AROUND THE CORNISH COAST; THAT'S WHY THE HARBOURS OF FISHING TOWNS SUCH AS PORTHLEVEN (SEEN HERE TAKING THE BRUNT OF A 100 MPH STORM) ARE BUILT OF SOLID GRANITE.

Did these shadowy figures from the past ever really stand on the clifftops of Hartland Point or the rocks of Land's End, luring ships onto the rocks with their lanterns in order to plunder the wrecks? Legend says so, but the tales probably sprang from the well-attested willingness of West Country coast-dwellers to rush down to the scene of an accidental shipwreck and salvage everything useful for themselves. Some locals undoubtedly put plunder before the welfare of the survivors, but far more often the story was of bravery and self-sacrifice in the effort to rescue wreck victims.

TREACHEROUS TEETH WAIT JUST BELOW THE SURFACE TO SEIZE AND CRUSH UNWARY SEAFARERS, AS AT HARTLAND POINT, NORTH DEVON, WITH ITS LONG JAGGED ROCK SCARS EXPOSED AT LOW TIDE.

A WILD JUMBLE OF NAKED ROCKS FORMS A VERY EVOCATIVE FULL STOP TO THE SOUTH-WEST PENINSULA, SLOPING DRAMATICALLY INTO THE SEA AT LAND'S END IN WESTERNMOST CORNWALL.

2 ■ THE WILD WEST
Torquay – Plymouth – Falmouth – Penzance – Isles of Scilly –
Newquay – Bude – Ilfracombe – Weston-super-Mare

The legends of the Wild West are variations of stories you'll hear elsewhere around the shores of Britain, but such tales seem to grow especially tall and wild in the salty air of the Cornish coast. The Land of Lyonesse, a wonderful walled city that lay in the sea between Land's End and the Isles of Scilly, was overwhelmed by the deep; its sole survivor the famed horseman Trevillian, who raced the tidal wave to land. Under the high dunes of Penhale Sands near Perranporth lies another fabulous city, golden Langarrow, smothered in a three-day sandstorm as punishment for the evil deeds of its inhabitants. And there was gold, too, in the throat of Matthew Trewhella of Zennor, whose song was so beautiful that it brought a mermaid from the sea to entice the young fisherman into the deep, there to sing for her forevermore.

Improbable? Maybe, but truth is sometimes stranger than fiction in a part of the world that can boast of a real historical character such as Parson Hawker of Morwenstow, who smoked opium in his cliff hut, pinched babies at the font to make them yell the devil out, and was once seen by his parishioners sitting on a rock singing to himself while disguised as a mermaid in a seaweed wig. Hawker was a real man of flesh-and-blood; at 19 he married a woman more than twice as old as he, and when he was 60 he wed a Polish girl only a third of his age (and had three children with her). Then there was Arthur, the once and future king, borne to Tintagel as a baby on the waves of a storm. Did he ever live and breathe? In the Wild West it's better to dream and speculate than to dig for that most boring of all commodities: hard fact.

WHEN THE SUN SHINES AND THE SEA ROLLS CALMLY IN TOWARDS PRISTINE SANDS UNDER BLUE SKIES, AS IN THIS VIEW OF LUGGER BAY NEAR PERRANPORTH, CORNWALL CAN SEEM THE MOST BEAUTIFUL PLACE ON EARTH.

Time and Tide

THE SEVERN ESTUARY TO CARDIGAN BAY

When it comes to the effects of tides, great and small, on the coastline of Britain, nowhere around the shores of these islands has a more intimate relation with the surge and pull of the sea than the 220 miles of savagely indented coast between the Severn bridges, high in the throat of the Severn Estuary, and the port of Fishguard, way out at the western extremity of Wales at the southern approaches to Cardigan Bay. The estuary of the Severn is a mighty waterway, stretching some 50 miles from the bridges near Bristol to the Glamorgan coast, where it swings westward and merges with the even broader tideway of the Bristol Channel. The Severn Estuary's tidal range is the second largest in the world. Spring tides can vary as much as 50 feet between high and low water, resulting in very strong currents, whirlpools and eddies, and the exposure of enormous areas of sand, mud and rocks at low water. Down the years, local fishermen, ferrymen and coasting seafarers have had to contend with the likelihood of being stranded or swept out to sea if they make any mistake in their reading of these immense and powerful tides.

As the flood tides of the Severn forge inland up the narrowing and twisting channel of the estuary, they become so constricted that the force of the sea's push causes the water at the rear of the surge to overtake the leading wave and build up a wall of water known as a 'bore', which travels inland at the speed of a cantering horse. Severn Bores are a daily occurrence, but most are so insignificant that they pass unnoticed. On about 130 days in each year they build to a wave worth watching, and exceptionally high tides at the spring and autumn equinoxes can sometimes produce really impressive bores – the highest recorded was over nine feet tall. Surfers and sailboarders try to ride these big bores, and by day there's often a carnival atmosphere

BY THE TIME IT HAS REACHED MAISEMORE BRIDGE SOME 30 MILES UPRIVER OF THE ESTUARY PROPER, A GOOD-SIZE SEVERN BORE IS A MAJESTIC SIGHT, A KINGLY TIDAL WAVE WITH SURFERS AND CANOEISTS FOR OUTRIDERS.

WHERE WATER AND LAND EMBRACE: THE MIGHTY RIVER SEVERN WINDS BETWEEN THE WELSH AND ENGLISH SHORES, A GREAT SNAKE OF POOLS, TIDE RIPS, SAND AND MUD BANKS THAT FORM A BEAUTIFUL, SUBTLY COLOURED MOSAIC.

3 ■ TIME AND TIDE
Bristol – Cardiff – Swansea – Llanelli – Tenby – Milford Haven –
Skokholm and Skomer Islands – St David's – Strumble Head

around the prime viewing locations just downstream of Gloucester, the tidal limit of the river. The best way to catch and appreciate the full majesty of a big Severn Bore, though, is to go to watch it on a moonlit night, when the foaming, hissing and rushing wall of water assumes a genuine majesty as it passes upriver.

Out in the wider estuary the tides rule the coast of South Wales. You sense their power in many different spheres – when you take a low-tide walk below the fractured cliffs of Nash Point and observe the high-tide mark many feet above your head; or as you pass the notice that warns of death by drowning on the rocky causeway to the tiny tidal islet of Sully Island; or when you search the rockpools of the Gower Peninsula at low tide and find spiky sea urchins, sea scorpions, large crabs and lobsters waiting in the shadows until the next flood unlocks their watery prisons. It was the tides that made a safe haven of Burry Holm's sandy islet for St Cenydd in the sixth century, and tides that forced the young Dylan Thomas to spend half the night at the seaward end of the Worm's Head promontory when they trapped him out there. Thomas loved the come-and-go of the sea, gazing with pleasure from the hut at Laugharne above the River Taf, where he wrote his poetry and plays as each tide made its incursion from Carmarthen Bay.

◀ THE GLAMORGAN HERITAGE COAST IS REMARKABLY UNSPOILED, BOTH INLAND ALONG THE PROTECTED COASTAL STRIP AND DOWN ON THE SHORE WHERE STRIATED CLIFFS SUCH AS THESE AT NASH POINT ARE WASHED BY THE PHENOMENALLY HIGH TIDES OF THE BRISTOL CHANNEL.

➤ THE COAST OF THE GOWER PENINSULA IS AMAZING FOR ITS MANY ROCKY PROMONTORIES; THEIR CREVICES HOLD THE BEST ROCKPOOLS IN WALES.

The great tides and winds of the estuary heaped and moulded the dunes at Kenfig Burrows near Port Talbot, and they smoothed the giant seven-mile beach at Pendine Sands to the west of Laugharne. Kenfig is now a National Nature Reserve, famous for its splendid wild orchids and other dune system flowers, and for the castle keep that marks the place under which the medieval town of Kenfig lies buried.

The immense beach at Pendine Sands is known for a burial, too – that of 'Babs', the Higham Special car powered by a 27-litre aero-engine in which John Parry-Thomas was killed in March 1927 while attempting to break the world land-speed record on the sands. Babs was buried in a pit dug into the beach immediately after the accident, and there she stayed until disinterred for restoration in 1969, to the dismay and active opposition of some of the locals.

Any proposal to disturb these South Wales sands and their secrets is capable of stirring up strong emotions, and none more so than schemes to dredge sand for commercial purposes from deposits off the Glamorgan and Pembrokeshire coast – sandbanks continually sculpted and shaped by the

THE 1927 WORLD LAND-SPEED RECORD ATTEMPT THAT CLAIMED THE LIFE OF JOHN PARRY-THOMAS WAS ONLY ONE OF MANY RUN ON THE LONG FLAT MILES OF PENDINE SANDS IN SOUTH WALES.

Bristol Channel tides, whose full force many of the coastal communities would feel if they were not shielded by the banks.

The vast natural harbour of Milford Haven at the south-western end of Pembrokeshire is one of the few really sheltered havens in Britain with the depth and space to handle king-sized tankers. It has become a major oil-refining and storage harbour, a role it manages to combine with being a tremendously valuable refuge for seabirds, fish and other marine organisms. One major oil spill has taken place – the leaking of some 70,000 tons of light crude from *Sea Empress* in 1996. Some would say that Milford Haven would be the last place in the world to make a good catch of fish, but in fact stocks have been recovering remarkably well and fishermen are catching lobster, crab, crayfish, bass, mullet, skate, scallops and shellfish.

A TANKER MAKES ITS WAY GINGERLY THROUGH THE NARROW WATERWAY OF MILFORD HAVEN, THE FINEST DEEPWATER INLET IN WALES, ALONG WHOSE SHORES WILD NATURE RUBS SHOULDERS WITH OIL TERMINALS AND REFINERIES.

West of Milford Haven, the mouth of the Bristol Channel widens towards the Irish Sea and the open Atlantic beyond. Here the influence of the strong tides finally begins to diminish. The spectacularly beautiful Pembrokeshire coast is itself a National Park, testimony to its beauty, wildlife and ecological value. Rugged cliffs guard some of the best beaches in Europe; the West Pembrokeshire sea may not be exactly tropical, but you would have to go a very long way around Britain to find better sands or more beautiful surroundings than at Marloes Sands, Broad Haven, Newgale Sands, Whitesands Bay and Abereiddi Bay.

And for anyone too restless to enjoy flopping out on the beach, one of the most scenic and enjoyable sections of the 186-mile Pembrokeshire Coast Path National Trail loops around the bays and leapfrogs the clifftops. There are many champion stretches of this beautiful path, a favourite among walkers with stamina and a feel for wild country. A real pearl is the walk from Whitesands Bay around St David's Head with its Iron Age fort, and on to climb to high ground from which on clear evenings you can make out the wave-like crests of the Wicklow Hills, nearly 100 miles away across the sea in Ireland.

THE STRATA OF BEACH ROCKS AND CLIFFS AT MARLOES SANDS ALL LIE CANTED AT THE SAME ANGLE, EVIDENCE OF TREMENDOUS SUBTERRANEAN UPHEAVALS THAT PUSHED AND TILTED WEST PEMBROKESHIRE HIGH OUT OF THE SEA.

SHORE PASTIMES ARE POPULAR AT NEWGALE BEACH – NOT JUST SWIMMING, SURFING AND SANDCASTLING, BUT THE EXCITING ACTIVITY OF KITE BUGGYING IN WHICH YOU LITERALLY RIDE THE WIND.

If you want to get really far away from it all, of course, there are the offshore islands of Pembrokeshire. Caldey Island off Tenby is the home of a community of Benedictine monks, while off the tip of the south-west Welsh peninsula lies a scatter of nature reserve islands accessible by small boat. Skokholm and Skomer are havens for breeding seabirds, especially the burrow-nesting Manx shearwaters, whose population in these two tiny islands alone reaches 150,000 or more. Further west lies Grassholm, home to 40,000 pairs of gannets. North of Skokholm and Skomer is rugged Ramsey Island, separated from the mainland by the tide-ripped channel of Ramsey Sound. So, in fact, it is tides that occupy us at the end, as at the start of this stretch of coast, as they sweep us north into the enormous arc of Cardigan Bay.

IT'S A LONGISH BOAT RIDE OUT TO GRASSHOLM, BUT WORTH IT JUST TO EXPERIENCE THE OVERWHELMING SOUND, SIGHT AND STENCH OF THE 80,000 GANNETS THAT THRONG THE LITTLE ISLAND.

THE VERY APTLY NAMED ELEPHANT ROCK DROOPS ITS LONG TRUNK OF ROCK INTO THE SEA OFF RAMSEY ISLAND, AN RSPB RESERVE WHERE YOU HAVE A GOOD CHANCE OF SPOTTING THE RARE RED-LEGGED CHOUGH.

The Travellers' Coast

CARDIGAN BAY TO THE WIRRAL PENINSULA

If the coastline from the Severn bridges to the west of Pembrokeshire is bound up with tides and the inward push of the sea, the great 200-mile sweep of seaboard that takes you from the southern shores of Cardigan Bay to the Dee Estuary and the blunt-tipped peninsula of the Wirral is all about the outward impulse. This is truly a travellers' coast, with ports and harbours that have seen the comings and goings of explorers, deep-sea sailors and fishermen, heroes real and mythical, master mariners, refugees, emigrants and ordinary people making everyday journeys. The hinterland of most of this vast tract of mid and north Wales is sparsely populated; all the action is down on the coast where fishing villages cling to rocky coves, and ports spring up and die back as the changing needs of the passing centuries dictate.

Ever since passengers first began to travel to Ireland for business and pleasure, they have been embarking at the sheltered deep-water port of Fishguard, at the western edge of Pembrokeshire. However, it wasn't until the Great Western Railway built a proper breakwater and railway pier at the beginning of the twentieth century that regular ferry services to Rosslare in south-east Ireland could begin. Before then, the town's main claim to fame was as the setting in 1797 for the last 'successful' invasion of Britain – successful only in the sense that the attackers, a French and Irish force of a thousand or so bewildered jailbirds and prisoners-of-war under the command of a septuagenarian American, did manage to scramble ashore. But that was as far as they got. Their attempt to conquer Britain ended in ignominious surrender

ONE OF STENA SEALINK'S BIG FERRIES OFF FISHGUARD IN WEST PEMBROKESHIRE. IRELAND IS ONLY FOUR HOURS AWAY THESE DAYS – LESS THAN TWO IF YOU OPT FOR ONE OF THE NEW HIGH-SPEED FERRIES.

to a much smaller force of defenders accompanied by the women of Fishguard, whose red cloaks and squat black hats were mistaken by the invaders for the uniforms of redcoat troops. So says the story, anyway.

What local seafarers achieved in the way of voyages to the ends of the earth can be seen neatly summed up in the memorials to master mariners, ships' carpenters and seamen in country churchyards up and down the coast. Aberaeron has a fine collection, as does Llanbadarn Fawr near Aberystwyth. A church census of 1681 shows that a third of the men in the tiny Flintshire coast parish of Llanasa were seamen, and Llanasa was fairly typical. Men from the coast of West Wales sailed all over the world, and the lives of those who stayed at home were usually bound up with the sea in one way or another: sailmakers, ships' coopers, boatswains, ships' chandlers and dozens of other salt trades, as parish records tell us. These professional seamen were (and are) well represented among the crews working the Irish ferries on the Fishguard to Rosslare route, as are those from the Isle of Anglesey port of Holyhead over to Dublin and Dun Laoghaire.

ABERAERON WAS A PLANNED TOWN, BROUGHT INTO BEING EARLY IN THE NINETEENTH CENTURY BY THE REVEREND ALBAN THOMAS JONES, WHO INHERITED £150,000 AND DREAMED BIG ABOUT ESTABLISHING A GREAT TRADING PORT.

The greatest of all West Wales's sea adventures is wrapped in a mist of historical uncertainty. The starting point is Borth-y-Gest on the Glaslyn Estuary near Criccieth, a tiny coastal settlement sited in the 'armpit' of Lleyn Peninsula that forms the upper arm of Cardigan Bay. The story goes that when King Owain Gwynedd ap Gruffydd died in 1170, his illegitimate son Prince Madog set sail from Borth-y-Gest, partly to go exploring and partly to escape the inevitable squabbling and bloodletting over the king's inheritance. Having discovered a 'distant and abundant land' far out across the western sea, Madog returned to Wales, loaded up with volunteer settlers, and forsook his native land for the new country he had found. This Welsh prince's voyage of discovery to the New World, if it really took place, would predate that of Christopher Columbus by more than

WAS IT PRINCE MADOG AP GRUFFYDD OR PRINCE MADOG THE CORMORANT WHO SET OFF FROM THIS QUIET NORTH WALES BAY TO FOUND A WELSH COLONY IN AMERICA? OR IS IT ALL JUST MYTH AND MOONSHINE? DREAM ON.

300 years. Unlikely? Perhaps – but not
so improbable, you would think, as the
suggestion that the adventure might actually
have taken place some 600 years earlier
under the leadership of another Prince
Madog, nicknamed 'The Cormorant', who
is said to have left Wales for lands across
the sea in the year 562 after a comet strike
had devastated large areas of Britain. Yet
recent DNA profiles of contemporary human
remains in the American Midwest, compared
with similar material in Wales, seem to point
to a genetic link between these people.
Fascinating stuff.

Many of the journeys associated with the
Travellers' Coast had the region itself as their
destination. Three great estuaries cut down
from the mountains into Cardigan Bay: Dyfi,
just north of Aberystwyth; Glaslyn, near the
root of the Lleyn Peninsula; and Mawddach,
in the middle. These estuaries, each of
their mouths composed of a mile or more
of treacherous sands amid shifting rivers and
tides, were dangerous places to cross, and
hundreds of lives were lost over the centuries
as travellers took risky shortcuts across the
tidal grounds. The coming of the railways in
the mid-Victorian era not only opened up
ports such as Fishguard and Holyhead to the
ferry trade, it also did away with the dangers
of travelling to and along the coast.

THE BROAD AND SANDY MAWDDACH ESTUARY CURVES
SPECTACULARLY OUT INTO CARDIGAN BAY. A FOOTPATH ALONG
A DISUSED RAILWAY LINE SHADOWS THE SOUTHERN SHORE OF
THE ESTUARY – A BEAUTIFUL WALK

The trains brought holidaymakers to the seaside in huge numbers. In 1851 the town of Aberystwyth, at the centre of the great curve of Cardigan Bay, was no more than a big village of just over 1000 houses. Its connection with the sea was almost entirely commercial – more than 200 ships were registered there, employing nearly 1000 men and boys. A chalybeate (iron salt) spring gave the town a healthy spa trade, but it was still difficult and occasionally dangerous to reach by bad mountain roads. After the arrival of the railway in 1864 the focus began to shift away from the harbour and spa onto the fine golden sands. Hotels sprang up, bathing machines proliferated, music halls opened their doors. Within 20 years the town was a thriving working-class seaside resort catering for enormous numbers of coal miners and steel workers and their families from the South Wales Valleys who could afford the money and time to travel there for a holiday on third-class railway tickets.

Much the same thing happened at Llandudno, Rhyl and Colwyn Bay on the North Wales coast, the favoured destinations of Liverpudlian holidaymakers; and also at Barmouth on the Mawddach Estuary, a great resort for Midlanders. Here a tremendous railway viaduct half a mile long straddles the estuary on 114 timber pile legs, one more

LLANDUDNO'S 1400-FOOT-LONG PIER HAS A BEND IN THE MIDDLE AND IS A MARVEL OF HIGH VICTORIAN STRUCTURAL ENGINEERING. YOU CAN CATCH A PLEASURE TRIP TO THE ISLE OF MAN FROM THE PIER.

ALL THE TECHNOLOGICAL WONDERS OF RHYL'S 'CHILDREN'S VILLAGE' ENTERTAINMENT COMPLEX CAN'T REPLACE THE SIMPLE ENJOYMENT CHILDREN GET FROM DOING WHAT THEY'VE ALWAYS DONE ON THE BEACH – PERFORMING HANDSTANDS AND BRAVING THE WAVES.

BEACHES, A PIER, SENSATIONAL ROCKPOOLING, A FINE OLD CLIFF RAILWAY AND A PLETHORA OF EXTRAVAGANT VICTORIAN HOTELS – ABERYSTWYTH MAY BE A CENTRE FOR WELSH LANGUAGE AND POLITICS, BUT IT'S ALSO A SPLENDID SEASIDE RESORT.

IT'S NOT ONLY TRAINS THAT CROSS BARMOUTH VIADUCT – CYCLISTS AND PEDESTRIANS USE
THE WOODEN-LEGGED VICTORIAN STRUCTURE AS A SHORT CUT ACROSS THE MOUTH OF THE
MAWDDACH BETWEEN FAIRBOURNE AND BARMOUTH.

entry in the long list of bold strokes of Victorian engineering genius.
Great technology made travellers of the masses; and yet back in
medieval times, pilgrims came this way in their tens of thousands,
some on horseback, others with only their legs to help them as they
faced down the rugged Lleyn Peninsula towards Bardsey. Also known
as the Island of 20,000 Saints – Bardsey is the place where St David
was said to have died – the tiny island off the tip of Lleyn has always
held a unique place in Welsh hearts. Some say that 20,000 pilgrims lie
buried there – travellers to unearthly destinations.

In these more secular days, walkers on the rugged Pilgrims Trail still make
their way out towards the seaward edge of Wales, to cross the sound
to Bardsey and puzzle over the mounds and stones of the Island of
20,000 Saints – still obeying the ancient impulse of the Travellers' Coast.

THE SLEEPING-OTTER SHAPE OF BARDSEY SIGNIFIED JOURNEY'S END TO PILGRIMS
THROUGHOUT THE MIDDLE AGES, AS THEY MADE THEIR WAY TO THE SACRED ISLAND
OF 20,000 SAINTS OFF THE ATLANTIC TIP OF THE LLEYN PENINSULA.

Shifting Sands

THE WIRRAL PENINSULA TO THE SOLWAY FIRTH

Looking at the coastline of Britain on a map or from the air, nothing about it appears to change from one year's end to the next. The bulge of East Anglia, the inward scoop of the Solent, the spindly arm of the Lleyn Peninsula and the great double 'v' of east coast Scotland seem fixed in their familiar shapes. Yet it's all an illusion. Coasts are, in fact, dynamic entities, constantly giving to or taking from the sea, eternally reinventing themselves, grain by grain and inch by inch. That process is seen to especially dramatic effect along the section of coastline between Liverpool and Carlisle in the north-west of England, where the country's most extensive tidal sands lie, moulding and remoulding their shapes and watercourses as the sea flows to cover them and ebbs away twice every 24 hours.

This continual development and change is not just a hydrological or geological phenomenon. Facing west towards Ireland, and way beyond to America, this is a coast on which the tides of human history and of social change have risen and receded – nowhere more so than in the port of Liverpool. The most striking factor in the city's history of the last few hundred years has been the influence of the Irish.

Liverpool is nearer to Dublin than it is to London, and has always had a healthy Irish population. Before Ireland's disastrous potato famine of 1845–9, the Irish accounted for some 17 per cent of the population, but by 1851 that figure had risen to 22 per cent. In the worst year of

THE GIANT PORT OF LIVERPOOL BUILDING, THE CUNARD BUILDING
AND THE ROYAL LIVER BUILDING TOPPED WITH ITS PERCHING
LIVER BIRDS – THESE GRAND EXPRESSIONS OF LIVERPOOL'S
COMMERCIAL GRANDEUR STAND AT THE PIER HEAD.

LIT BY THE SETTING SUN AS IT DIPS INTO THE ATLANTIC, THE RIBBED SANDS OF CROSBY BEACH MARK THE START OF THE GREAT 20-MILE SYSTEM OF DUNES AND SANDS KNOWN AS THE SEFTON COAST.

ILLUMINATED FOR THE EVENING'S FUN, THE FLASH AMUSEMENT PALACES OF BLACKPOOL'S GOLDEN MILE WINK AND SPARKLE IN THE SHADOW OF THE 518-FOOT-HIGH BLACKPOOL TOWER. LISTEN! IS THAT THE MIGHTY WURLITZER?

the famine, 1847, some 300,000 Irish immigrants poured into Liverpool. But at the same time they were flooding away from the city towards America – 200,000 per year in 1845 and 1846. All in all, between 1830 and 1930, around nine million Irish people left Liverpool for the New World – the equivalent of the entire pre-Famine population of Ireland. Such an enormous throughput was bound to have its effect on the city. Famous Liverpudlians with Irish roots are more numerous than knobs on a shillelagh. For example, without the Irish

connection the city would never have given birth to the Beatles: John Lennon's great-grandmother came from Omagh in County Tyrone, while Paul McCartney's grandfather was a Monaghan man and George Harrison's grandpa hailed from Wexford.

The great sands of the coast begin just north of Liverpool at Crosby, continuing in a broad arc round to the Ribble Estuary and on by way of Blackpool and Heysham into the giant sand saucer of Morecambe Bay and the vast sand flats of the Duddon Estuary in south

THE DULL YELLOW DUNES AT AINSDALE HIDE A NATURAL
TREASURE HOUSE; IN THIS NATIONAL NATURE RESERVE OF
1255 ACRES THRIVE 460 PLANT SPECIES, NATTERJACK TOADS,
SAND LIZARDS AND RED SQUIRRELS.

Lakeland. The 20-mile shore that stretches in a convex arc from Crosby
to Southport and the River Ribble is known as the Sefton Coast and
contains England's largest system of sand dunes. This long range of
sandhills is part of an ever-changing coast that grew seaward by
1000 feet in the eighteenth and early nineteenth centuries. It was
helped by local landowners who planted stabilizing marram grass and
built sand-trap fences, then lost it all during the following century-and-
a-half, due to an increase in stormy weather and in dredging and
dumping operations in Liverpool Bay. Now the dunes are beginning
to build again in places. Their finely tuned and unique flora includes
rare orchids, dune helleborines and such exotics as smooth cat's-ear

and Isle of Man cabbage. Long, flat sandy beaches lie between dunes
and sea. It was on the sands at Southport that Red Rum, much-loved
triple winner of the Grand National, took his training runs.

Sands and muds combine to form great banks at the marshy mouth of
the River Lune as it snakes to the sea from Lancaster. Beyond here the
sands spread out at low tide into the enormous wastes of Morecambe
Bay, where 117 square miles of sand lie exposed on the ebb. To reach
the edge of the sea from the resort of Grange-over-Sands at extreme
low tide, you would have to walk ten miles out across the sands. Not
that you would try any such thing on your own because Morecambe Bay

5 ■ SHIFTING SANDS
Liverpool – Southport – Preston – Blackpool – Morecambe –
Barrow-in-Furness – Ravenglass – Whitehaven

at low tide is one of the most dangerous places in Britain. Three rivers snake through the sands – the Kent, Leer and Leven – and they are unpredictable waters, especially the Kent, which has been known to switch from one side of the bay to the other in the space of a couple of days. Other hidden streams run under the sands, forming quicksands and soft sinking pits. Sandbanks appear and disappear, change shape, rise and fall from one tide to the next. Out in the middle you can get lost, disorientated, benighted or marooned on a sandbank amid rising waters. When the tide comes in, it does so far more quickly than a panicking person can flee. On the night of 5 February 2004 a party of immigrant Chinese workers was caught by the tide and 21 were drowned – the worst recorded single incident of tragedy among the hundreds of unwise or unfortunate victims who have been drowned in the bay down the centuries.

◄ THE TIDES OF MORECAMBE BAY ARE TREACHEROUS FOR WALKERS AND CAR DRIVERS ALIKE. IT'S TEMPTING TO MOTOR OUT ACROSS THE SANDS AND PARK BY THE EDGE OF THE WATER, BUT YOU CAN VERY QUICKLY FIND THAT YOU'RE MAROONED IN A FAST-RISING SEA.

➤ A GROUP OF WALKERS, ABLY LED BY THE SANDS GUIDE, MAKES A SAFE CROSSING OF THE TREACHEROUS SANDS OF MORECAMBE BAY. THOSE WHO GO IT ALONE RISK BEING CUT OFF AND DROWNED BY THE INCOMING TIDE.

The Chinese workers were collecting cockles, which cling to the rocks and lie under the sands in uncountable millions. Along with mussels, shrimps and marine worms, they make a vast larder of Morecambe Bay for the wading birds that throng here – knot, dunlin, curlew, godwit, oystercatcher. The bay is paradise for birdwatchers, and it is a great place for walkers, too, but only under the careful guidance of the handful of local experts who know the intricacies of the sands inside out. Cedric Robinson, the official Sands Guide, is out in the bay at all hours checking the 'brobs' or laurel sprig markers that he places to identify the safe routes across the sands. He leads parties of all sizes on walks across Morecambe Bay – a memorable experience, but emphatically not one to be undertaken by unguided walkers.

The sands of time have entirely altered the shape of work and play along this coast. Fishing still takes place, albeit on a much diminished scale: deep-sea trawling from Fleetwood near Blackpool, and inshore fishing from smaller ports such as Workington and Maryport, which lie further north among the fine red sandstone cliffs of the Cumbrian coast. Netsmen still take their long nets out into the Solway Firth for the 'haaf fishing', in hopes of catching a salmon. But it was mineral mining and working that made the fortune of much of the coast: coal from the pits around Whitehaven, and ironstone from up in the Lake District hills that fed ironworks at Millom and Askam on the Duddon Estuary just round the corner from Morecambe Bay. A great bank of steel slag known as Askam Pier still sticks way out into the estuary as witness to the long-dead industry.

Nowadays the future seems more futuristic than ever. Barrow-in-Furness builds nuclear submarines, and Whitehaven refurbishes its Georgian streets from the coffers of British

FLEETWOOD FISH DOCK IN 1983, WITH THREE TYPICAL FLEETWOOD TRAWLERS OF THE DAY TIED UP BULWARK TO BULWARK. FISHING RESTRICTIONS FOLLOWING THE ICELAND 'COD WARS' OF THE 1970s AND QUOTA CUTBACKS IN THE 1980s AND 1990s HAVE VASTLY REDUCED THE FISHING FLEET.

5 ■ SHIFTING SANDS
Liverpool – Southport – Preston – Blackpool – Morecambe – Barrow-in-Furness – Ravenglass – Whitehaven

Nuclear Fuels Ltd, the town's main employer at its nearby Sellafield reprocessing plant. But down on Sunderland Point, a bleak spit of land at the mouth of the River Lune, a few sandstone warehouses of the Georgian era bear witness to the extraordinary past; for it was here on this lonely promontory that the very first bale of raw cotton from America was landed, the opening act in the Industrial Revolution that changed the face of Britain for ever.

BIG CRANES ON WHITEHAVEN HARBOUR: BUT THESE DAYS MOST TOWNSFOLK WORK IN THE CHEMICAL OR NUCLEAR INDUSTRIES, AND THE WEST CUMBRIAN TOWN IS LOOKING MORE AND MORE TO TOURISM BASED ON ITS SUPERB GEORGIAN ARCHITECTURE.

Between a Rock and a Hard Place

NORTHERN IRELAND: CARLINGFORD LOUGH TO LOUGH FOYLE

From Greencastle, out at the tip of Lough Foyle in northernmost
County Donegal, the southward view over the water into Northern
Ireland is of County Derry's low-lying shore of muddy, tidal marshes
and sandy beaches, bird-haunted and beckoning across the narrow
jaws of the sea lough. It's even better, but entirely different, down at
the opposite end of the Province. Among the green hills of the Tain
Peninsula in County Louth in the Irish Republic, a track climbs from
Windy Gap up to the saddle of ground between the peaks of Barnavave
and Slieve Foy. Gazing north from here across Carlingford Lough
into County Down, you are struck by the magnificent prospect of the
Mountains of Mourne. You'd have to go a long way to beat that, surely?
Well, not all that far – not if you're coming in by ferry from Heysham or
Liverpool or the Isle of Man, with the low green hills and sandy shores
of the Ards Peninsula as a bonus. Crossing the North Channel from
Stranraer? That's the best of the lot, of course, because then you see
the great multicoloured cliffs of the Antrim coast growing out of the
sea like the flanks of a sea monster hauling itself up from the deep.

The coast of Northern Ireland is one of singular beauty and drama.
Any country would be proud of a coastal feature such as the
Mountains of Mourne with their green and purple slopes running
down to the sea. But variety is the spice of this coast. North of the
Mournes, the County Down coast rounds out into the blunt little
Lecale Peninsula with its cliffs and coves, and then bulges north into
the far larger and more striking peninsula of the Ards, which hangs

THE DARK, SHAPELY PEAKS OF THE MOURNE MOUNTAINS CHALLENGE AND
ENTICE EVERY WALKER WHO LAYS EYES ON THEM. ANYONE WHO VENTURES
AMONG THE MOURNES WILL FIND THEM UNCROWDED, EASILY MANAGEABLE
AND BLESSED WITH SENSATIONAL VIEWS FROM THE SUMMITS.

6 ■ BETWEEN A ROCK AND A HARD PLACE
Newcastle – Belfast – Carrickfergus – Larne – Ballycastle –
Portrush – Portstewart – Derry

out and down from the great indentation of Belfast Lough like a gently bent arm. Between the peninsular 'arm' and the mainland 'body' – in the armpit of County Down, so to speak – lies the long inlet of Strangford Lough, a tidal fiord some 20 miles long that is a birdwatchers' heaven. To the enormous invertebrate larder of the lough, especially in winter, come wading birds and wildfowl in their many thousands – lapwing and godwit, golden and ringed plover, shelduck, pintail and wigeon, and around 12,000 light-bellied brent geese from Greenland, some ten per cent of the entire world population of these small but hardy birds.

Belfast sits at the inner end of its lough like a spider in a web of roads and dock quays. From here, County Down gives place to County Antrim. It's a 50-mile stretch from Larne to the Giant's Causeway, and the drama of the coastline keeps growing the further north you travel. The cliffs of Antrim form the most breathtaking piece of coastal scenery in the whole of Ireland, reaching as high as 800 feet and presenting a breathtaking array of colours: creamy limestone, dark red sandstone and pale grey puddingstone. But it's the purple-hued basalt that is the rock star hereabouts, running down to the sea in a succession of dramatic,

◄ COUNTLESS BAYS AND DOZENS OF ISLETS MAKE UP THE GREAT SEA LOUGH OF STRANGFORD LOUGH, A HAVEN FOR EARLY CHRISTIAN HERMITS IN THE DARK AGES, THESE DAYS A REFUGE FOR WILDFOWL BY THE HUNDRED THOUSAND.

➤ THE CLIFFS OF THE ANTRIM COAST ARE FAMOUS FOR THEIR GREAT HEIGHT AND THEIR DRAMATICALLY COLOURED AND SHAPED ROCKS, BUT THEIR TURF ALSO NURTURES WILD FLOWERS, INCLUDING BIG CLUMPS OF SEA PINKS.

sharp-prowed headlands and cliffs. They are formed of solidified lava, overspill from some vast volcanic explosion at the end of the dinosaur era some 60 million years ago. Their flanks are deeply cut by nine river valleys, the famed Glens of Antrim, into whose rugged mouths a yachtsman passing up the coast can look, one after the other.

From Ballycastle, it's a tourist coast round to the Giant's Causeway, Northern Ireland's premier tourist attraction. Dr Johnson's terse little aphorism – 'Worth seeing, but not worth going to see' – might not be too well liked by the tourist board, but it pretty neatly fits the bill. Coming up the coast from the south you'll be surfeited with scenic wonders by the time you reach the 37,000 hexagonal stumps of cooled basalt that slope into the sea in a blunt-nosed promontory below the cliffs. The Causeway is best seen in a winter storm with gale-driven waves bursting across it and sheets of spray shredding into mist. From here the cliffs gradually decline in height towards the long north-facing beaches of Magilligan Point and the wide tidal slobs or mud flats and marshes of the County Down shore of Lough Foyle – more prime birdwatching territory.

GEOLOGISTS SAY THAT RAPIDLY COOLING BASALT FORMED THE HEXAGONAL COLUMNS OF THE GIANT'S CAUSEWAY; ROMANTICS INSIST IT WAS THE GIANT HERO FIONN MACCUMHAILL (FINN McCOOL) WHO BUILT THE CAUSEWAY AS A MEANS OF GETTING OVER TO THE HEBRIDEAN ISLAND OF STAFFA TO SEE HIS GIANTESS GIRLFRIEND.

6 ■ BETWEEN A ROCK AND A HARD PLACE
Newcastle – Belfast – Carrickfergus – Larne – Ballycastle – Portrush – Portstewart – Derry

You could certainly cruise this beautiful coast without guessing at the hard and troubled times it has seen. But a little dip into the history books, and a dollop of imagination as you look around, will soon uncover the realities behind the breathtaking scenery. Along a coast open to privateers, invaders and ill-disposed neighbours, particularly in a country whose allegiances have been so keenly contested for so long, it has been a way of life for the inhabitants to watch, ward and guard against unwelcome visitors. Witnesses to this 'have-and-hold' attitude include huge, grim-looking Norman castles such as the Antrim strongholds of Carrickfergus and Dunluce, and stark stone tower houses like the fifteenth-century Kilclief Castle in County Down. And fears of a seaborne assault by a foreign power seemed to be borne out in 1588 when the invasion fleet of the Spanish Armada sailed by – except that the galleons were being harried towards wreck by destructive gales. On 30 October the galleon *Girona,* laden with around 1200 men, struck Lacada Point near the Giant's Causeway and sank with the loss of all but a handful of survivors – perhaps as few as three. Her fabulous golden treasure, salvaged from 1967 to 1969, is displayed in Belfast's Ulster Museum, but there is no memorial to the victims on the spot where they died.

THE GREAT NORMAN KEEP OF CARRICKFERGUS, BUILT 90 FEET HIGH IN 1180, STILL DOMINATES SEA AND LAND FROM ITS ROCK AT THE ENTRANCE TO BELFAST LOUGH. IN SPITE OF CAPTURES AND SIEGES, CARRICKFERGUS REMAINED IN MILITARY USE UNTIL THE EARLY TWENTIETH CENTURY.

MAN AND THE ELEMENTS HAVE INTERVENED TO SPECTACULAR EFFECT IN THE FORTUNES OF DUNLUCE CASTLE. IN 1584 DUNLUCE WAS CAPTURED BY AN IRISH FORCE THAT HAULED UP THE CLIFFS IN BASKETS; IN 1639 A PORTION OF THE CASTLE CRASHED INTO THE SEA DURING A TERRIBLE STORM.

THE ECCENTRIC BUT WARM-HEARTED PROTESTANT BISHOP OF LONDONDERRY AND 4TH EARL OF BRISTOL, FREDERICK HERVEY, BUILT THE MUSSENDEN TEMPLE IN 1783. HE MAY HAVE INSTALLED A MISTRESS; HE CERTAINLY ALLOWED LOCAL CATHOLICS TO CELEBRATE MASS THERE, A GRAVE OFFENCE IN THOSE DAYS.

Strife was commonplace between the local people and the Scots and English-born incomers who 'planted' the ancient Province of Ulster from the early seventeenth century onwards. You'll find evidence in the strength and thickness of the walls that encircle the old city of Derry, and in local tales of brutality and derring-do – these include the throwing of locals off the Gobbin cliffs by a vengeful party of soldiers from Carrickfergus garrison in 1641, and Sorley Boy MacDonnell's famous 1584 capture of Dunluce Castle from the English when he had his men hauled up the cliffs in baskets to take the defenders by surprise.

Scars of old hardships last long hereabouts, too. When the coast road that loops the Antrim cliffs so spectacularly was built in the 1830s, hungry and poverty-stricken local men were offered the work to earn some money. And when the 22-mile-long wall was built between 1904 and 1922 to enclose the reservoirs of the Mourne Mountains, it was poor men with hungry families who were selected to construct the wall that still connects the high peaks and passes of those mountains. But perhaps it's the local tales of heroes and villains that will last the longest: the eccentric Bishop of Londonderry, who was said to keep one of his mistresses in Mussenden Temple on the Derry cliffs, the naughty Bishop of Down, who was defrocked for living in sin with a married woman in Kilclief Castle, the notorious witches of Island Magee, and of course that popular boatman of Rathlin Island, who would uncork a bottle of whisky for favoured customers as they made the crossing, toss the stopper into the sea and invite them to join him in drinking the bottle out before they touched land again.

FULMARS, RAZORBILLS, PUFFINS, GUILLEMOTS, KITTIWAKES AND GULLS BY THE HUNDRED THOUSAND PACK EVERY LEDGE AND CREVICE OF THE CLIFFS ON RATHLIN ISLAND IN THE BREEDING SEASON.

The Battleground Coast
THE SOLWAY FIRTH TO THE ISLE OF SKYE

A glance at the map of the West of Scotland tells you all about the character of this stunningly dramatic, remote and wildly beautiful battleground of a coast. From the Rhinns of Galloway down in the south-west – a hammerhead peninsula of sandstone that will be an island when the Atlantic has finished smashing it free – to the ragged mountains and wind-blasted beaches of the Western Isles, the entire seaboard bears witness to the violent clash between sea and land. This eternal battle pits the irresistible force of the hungry Atlantic against the immoveable object of the volcanic rocks, the granite and sandstone of the mainland coast and the islands.

The Atlantic is winning the contest, rock by rock and grain by grain. It has cut the western Scottish coast into tatters, ripped great sea lochs into it, gouged out bays and fiords, severed land from land, made peninsulas of solid land and islands of peninsulas. As for the islands – thousands are scattered in the face of the Atlantic, head on to its endlessly east-sweeping waves and winds. A few dozen support human settlements, but most are empty hummocks and platforms of rock where not even the most self-denying of hermits could scratch an existence.

The unceasing battle between sea and land has spawned a supplementary skirmish, one that has occupied only the blink of an eye in geological time – that between man and the harsh west coast environment. On the mainland with its ferocious winter gales, its thin soils and steep, boggy slopes, things are tough enough. Out on the islands they are generally a lot tougher. Even today, with all the support that modern ferries and planes offer, island communities can be cut off for weeks at a time when the weather grows teeth. And if accident or illness bereaves a small island community, it does not just deprive a family of their breadwinner or a school of its teacher; each islander has multiple jobs, multiple responsibilities, and the loss of one person leaves a far larger gap than in most mainland communities. To make a home and a life for yourself and your family in such a place has always required endurance, practicality, stoicism and a sense of humour.

Memorials to this conflict between man and place can be seen up and down the Battleground Coast. Sometimes people are compelled to retreat, leaving only traces of their settlements behind them – as with the

A SOLITARY PUFFIN (MOST UNUSUAL FOR THIS SOCIABLE SPECIES) STANDS SENTINEL ON THE THIN TURF OF THE TRESHNISH ISLES, A GROUP OF BASALT LEDGES AND PLUGS RISING OUT OF THE SEA BETWEEN COLL AND THE ISLE OF MULL.

harsh and lonely Treshnish Islands
in the sound between Mull and Tiree,
abandoned some time in the nineteenth
century, or the remote Atlantic outpost
of St Kilda, 40 miles west of the Outer
Hebridean archipelago, whose hardy
but ageing inhabitants petitioned to
be evacuated in 1930 when life had
become too hard.

ON THE MIGHTY CLIFFS OF ST KILDA THE ISLAND
CRAGSMEN WOULD SCRAMBLE FEARLESSLY TO SNARE
SEABIRDS AND GATHER THEIR EGGS, VITAL SOURCES
OF FOOD FOR PEOPLE SURVIVING IN THIS HARSH
AND ISOLATED ENVIRONMENT.

BEACHES AS UNSPOILED
AND BEAUTIFUL AS THIS
ONE AT BACK OF KEPPOCH
NEAR ARISAIG IN SOUTH
MORAR ARE WIDESPREAD
AROUND THE REMOTE
PENINSULAS OF THE
WESTERN HIGHLANDS.

A THATCHED CROFT HOUSE
IN TRADITIONAL STYLE,
FACING THE OPEN ATLANTIC
ON THE ISLE OF TIREE. THICK
WALLS, TINY WINDOWS
AND DOORS, AND A GOOD
SNUG THATCH ALL HELP
TO KEEP THE WIND AND
SALT SPRAY OUT.

Sometimes it is man who forces the advantage: witness the lighthouses built during the nineteenth century in such remote and dangerous places as Skerryvore, 11 miles out from the Isle of Tiree, and Oigh-sgeir, away to the West of the Isle of Rhum. Some isolated coastal regions abandoned by the locals as uninhabitable, such as parts of the peninsulas of Morar and Knoydart, are now being repopulated by incomers with enough private income or a reliable enough home-based industry to have a try at making a living and settling in. But even in fishing villages and crofting areas provided with sufficient shelter and modern communications, the daily struggle between man and place goes on.

LIFE ON THE WEST COAST OF SCOTLAND CAN BE VERY HARSH AND DEMANDING; THAT'S WHY PEOPLE TURN TO AND HELP EACH OTHER, AS WITH THESE MEN CLEARING CARGO TOGETHER FROM A JETTY IN KNOYDART.

THE TRIANGULAR DESIGN
AND MOATED SITE OF
CAERLAVEROCK CASTLE
DIDN'T PREVENT ITS
CAPTURE BY KING EDWARD
LONGSHANKS IN 1300,
AND MANY SUBSEQUENT
CENTURIES OF SIEGES AND
BLOODSHED. BUT WHEN
THINGS BECAME CALMER
IN THE SEVENTEENTH
CENTURY, THE EARL OF
NITHSDALE BUILT A FINE
HOUSE WITHIN THE WALLS.

STORMS OVER THE WESTERN
SEA CAN BE SUDDEN AND
VIOLENT, AS WITH THIS ONE
AT LOCH NAN UAMH WITH
LIGHTNING FORKING INTO
THE SEA.

These battles between sea and land and between man and environment are impersonal, but this coast has also seen every kind of ramification of human conflict. Actual sword-on-sword battles have been thick on the ground, many of them concerned with the ancient struggle between the Scots and the Auld Enemy from across their southern border. Castles that had been built by Scots lords for personal protection, such as the wonderful triangular stronghold built in 1277 by Lord Maxwell at Caerlaverock on the Solway Firth, were soon captured by the English, recaptured by the Scots, burned, besieged, and captured again and again. Robert the Bruce and a handful of men beat 2000 English soldiers on the Galloway slopes in 1307; Sir Thomas Wharton and his 3000 Englishmen beat 10,000 Scots and captured 1200 of them at Solway Moss in 1542. In July 1745 Bonnie Prince Charlie landed at Loch nan Uamh on the Ardnamurchan Peninsula to lead the last hurrah of the clans against the English nine months later at the Battle of Culloden, where Scottish dreams of a Scottish king were shattered once and for all.

Battles and slaughter between the clans themselves, particularly
islanders, often reached a level of ferocity that left the England–
Scotland conflict looking like a tea party. When a party of
Macleod men from Harris raped some Macdonald girls on the Isle
of Eigg in 1577, they were caught, castrated and set adrift by the
Macdonald men. The Macleod clan responded by invading Eigg,
tracking the population to a cave that they had all fled to, and lighting
a smoky fire at the entrance. The smoke filled the cave and 'smorit
the haill people thairin to the number of 395 personnes, men, wife
and bairnis.' One islander survived. The Macdonalds repopulated
Eigg, only for the settlers to be completely wiped out again 11 years
later by a raiding party of Macleans from Mull led by Lachlan Maclean.
The Macdonalds got their revenge, although they had to wait ten more
years for it. In August 1598, on Macdonald land in the Isle of Islay, they
caught Lachlan Maclean and yet another marauding gang from Mull.
The Macleans took refuge in Kilnave Chapel on the shoes of Loch
Gruinart, whereupon their enemies set fire to the thatch of the church
and burned them all to death.

Even the savagery of clan versus clan paled into insignificance when
it came to religion in these parts. The Covenanters who made a bid
for religious freedom in the seventeenth century were shot or hanged
out of hand by the dragoons who hunted them in company with local
'gentlemen'. In the flat green marshes below Wigtown in south
Galloway, a granite pillar marks the spot where, on a May morning
in 1685, a woman in her sixties and a girl of 18 were tied to stakes
to drown in the incoming Solway tides. The graves of Margaret
McLachlan and Margaret Wilson lie in the churchyard just up the
hill, their tombstones inscribed in everlasting accusation with the
names of the men who condemned them to this horrible and lingering
death for 'non-conformity, disorderly behaviour, and absenteeism
from church' – in other words, for being Covenanters.

TWO BEAUTIFUL HUMPS: THE SHARP-FINNED BACK OF A MINKE
WHALE REPLICATES THE SHAPE OF AN SGURR, A GREAT SHEER-
SIDED BULGE OF COLUMNAR PITCHSTONE LAVA THAT
DOMINATES THE SOUTHERN HALF OF THE ISLE OF EIGG.

A GRANITE PILLAR MARKS THE SPOT WHERE IN MAY 1685 ELDERLY MARGARET MCLACHLAN AND TEENAGER MARGARET WILSON WERE TIED TO STAKES AND LEFT TO DROWN BECAUSE THEY WOULD NOT RENOUNCE THEIR COVENANTER FAITH.

Today's conflicts around the Battleground Coast tend to centre on matters of ecology and conservation. Should the building of a huge wind farm on the outer Hebridean Isle of Lewis go ahead, or the giant quarry in the flanks of Harris continue operations? Ought the people of Islay oppose the destruction of the island's peat bogs by machine-cutting? Should the Skye bridge have been built? Do the pollutant effects of fish farms outweigh the economic benefits? These are the new skirmishing grounds of this remote but vibrant coast, which many think is the most beautiful part of Britain – bar none. Striding among abandoned cultivation strips across a seemingly empty West Coast peninsula or sitting dreaming on a deserted Hebridean beach facing the Atlantic, it's easy to think of these shores as being at the end of their interaction with the human species, forever purged of people and their pollution. But constant vigilance from those who live and get their daily bread here, and from those who love the West and work for its well-being from afar, is the price paid for those clear green seas and that pristine silver sand.

THE SEA MAY BE COLD, BUT THE BEACHES AND HEADLANDS OF THE OUTER HEBRIDES ARE FABULOUSLY BEAUTIFUL, AS AT TRAIGH NA BERIE ON THE ISLE OF LEWIS.

Bare Bones and Standing Stones

THE ISLE OF SKYE TO THE SHETLAND ISLES

During the Second World War, a group of 550 Italian prisoners-of-war was incarcerated on the Orkney islet of Lamb Holm. These men from the sunny south, penned up on a weather-beaten blob of rock in a cold sea, set about expressing their homesickness and the strength of their religious faith by converting a couple of grimly functional Nissen huts into a replica of a Renaissance chapel of their homeland. An elaborate, crow-stepped frontage was formed. The delicate tracery of the sanctuary screen was made of wrought scrap-iron, the light fittings shaped out of Spam tins. The POWs carved a tabernacle out of driftwood, and painted plasterboard to resemble tiles.

From the barest of materials and out of the pooled talents of their fraternity these uprooted men created a tiny patch of Italy, an enclave of hope in the bleakest of situations. The Lamb Holm chapel, still open to the public, speaks volumes about the power of communities to transcend hardship by pulling together. That triumph of the human spirit over dire adversity, the very essence of the communities of Britain's most northerly outposts, is personified by the lonely Italians of Camp 60 in their dogged determination not to be beaten, their ingenuity, their strength of mind and heart.

Travelling north and east through the great arc of rugged coasts and islands that stretches from Skye to Shetland, you get the impression of a land stripped to its bare bones. The formations of the rocks themselves seem open and exposed to the elements. On the Isle of Skye, the dark, jagged gabbro of the Black Cuillins and the smoother, dusky granite of the neighbouring Red Cuillins stand naked against the clouds. The pink gneiss of the cliffs of Cape Wrath gleams through the spray of the storm waves that scour the headland where the Atlantic

DURING THE SECOND WORLD WAR, ITALIAN PRISONERS-OF-WAR IN ORKNEY BUILT THE CHAPEL ON LAMB HOLM ISLAND OUT OF TWO NISSEN HUTS AND SCAVENGED SCRAP MATERIAL, AS AN EXPRESSION OF FAITH AND HOPE IN ADVERSITY.

THE MAGNIFICENT GRANDEUR OF THE WESTERN HIGHLAND VOLCANIC MOUNTAIN SCENERY REACHES ITS APEX IN THE BLACK CUILLIN HILLS ON THE ISLE OF SKYE.

meets the North Sea. Though Orkney's sandstone underlies flowery shell-sand beaches and grassy swards, the thinness of the tree cover is very noticeable to a stranger; while up in the northernmost archipelago of Shetland, the granite glints darkly through all but the barest covering of peat and heather. The combination of unchecked gales and salt spray abolishes trees, blasts grazing and sweeps away all plants but the hardiest. If you want a flower garden or a sycamore grove in Shetland, you'll need to wall it round against salt and wind. The sight of a great sea stack such as the Old Man of Hoy, a slender pillar some 450 feet tall with its base in the sea off the Orkney island of Hoy, is a reminder of the power of these strong northern winds and waves to cut and crumble the toughest of rock; but it's also a testament to the endurance of those bared bones of the landscape in the face of the most elemental of elements around the British Isles.

RED GRANITE FORMS THE RED CUILLIN HILLS OF SKYE. IT WEATHERS INTO CHARACTERISTIC ROUND PROFILES, IN CONTRAST TO THE GABBRO THAT LENDS THE BLACK CUILLIN THEIR FORMIDABLE JAGGED OUTLINE.

TOPPING OUT ON THE 450-FOOT SANDSTONE PILLAR OF THE OLD MAN OF HOY REMAINS ONE OF THE PRIME CHALLENGES FOR ROCK CLIMBERS, WHO RECKON IT BRITAIN'S FINEST SEA STACK CLIMB.

8 ■ BARE BONES AND STANDING STONES
Isle of Skye – Isle of Lewis – Bettyhill – Thurso –
John O'Groats – Orkney Islands – Shetland Isles

The clan-based system of mutual obligation and interdependence evolved as a natural response to the daily challenge of working and living in such a harsh environment. And when that system broke down in the face of infiltration by more southerly and alien cultures, the people of these northern coasts and islands were subjected to a particularly brutal form of ethnic cleansing. During the late eighteenth and early nineteenth centuries, most of the land was bought up by outsiders more interested in making a profit from sheep farming than in the welfare of their tenants. Local inhabitants were forced from their homes, which were then torched; the people went to the coast to take up the unfamiliar work of fishing, or emigrated in droves to America or Canada, while the land they had farmed was put to sheep grazing. Some 15,000 people were cleared from the 1.5 million acres owned by the Duke of Stafford (later the Duke of Sutherland). One of these, the stonemason Donald Macleod of Rosal, wrote passionately of the destruction and misery he had witnessed in Strathnaver, a narrow glen that runs to Scotland's most northerly coast:

'The consternation and confusion were extreme. Little or no time was given for the removal of persons or property; the people striving to remove the sick and the helpless before the fire should reach them; next, struggling to save the most valuable of their effects. The cries of the women and children, the roaring of the affrighted cattle, hunted at the same time by the yelling dogs of the shepherds amid the smoke and fire, altogether presented a scene that completely baffles description, it required to be seen to be believed.'

Hundreds of communities were destroyed. But the spirit of the people survived. Like their forefathers, today's Highlanders and islanders are resilient and hospitable people. The warmth shown to the stranger, the cup of tea at the house door, the dram of whisky and the invitation in for a bit of a chat are endemic – old-fashioned attitudes, maybe, but alive and well in a region still so unaffected by petty crime that its inhabitants can leave their front doors permanently on the latch and their bicycles propped against the garden wall. Traditional music, that thermometer of a community's social health, is thriving. Bagpipers play in the pubs of Skye and the back rooms of Sutherland. Shetland fiddle music has never been more widespread through the generations. Idiosyncrasies are the norm; the woman who covers her house with shells, the man who sings to the seals, the Foula islanders who still scorn this new-fangled Christmas and celebrate Auld Yule on 6 January.

LOOKING EAST OVER THE PALE SANDS OF SANGOBEG BAY TOWARDS WHITEN HEAD ON THE
NORTH-WEST COAST OF SCOTLAND.

Isle of Skye – Isle of Lewis – Bettyhill – Thurso –
John O'Groats – Orkney Islands – Shetland Isles

The Scots of the north live surrounded by monuments of their deep history. These striking structures fall into two groups – tombs of various kinds, and other formations of standing stones whose purpose remains obscure. The Orkney archipelago is especially rich in both. On the principal island of Orkney Mainland, the green mound of Maes Howe contains Europe's finest chambered tomb, an awe-inspiring 5000-year-old 'cathedral of death'. Other magnificent Orcadian tombs include the Tomb of the Eagles on South Ronaldsay, a clifftop mausoleum where humans and eagles were buried together, the Dwarfie Stane on

THE SLEEPY LITTLE HARBOUR OF PORTREE SHELTERS FISHING BOATS, PLEASURE YACHTS, THE SKYE LIFEBOAT AND THE CRAFT OF ISLANDERS VISITING TOWN FROM REMOTE WATERSIDE COMMUNITIES ELSEWHERE ON THE ISLAND.

THE INNOCENT GREEN HILLOCK OF MAES HOWE ON ORKNEY MAINLAND CONCEALS THE FINEST CHAMBERED TOMB IN EUROPE, A STONE-BUILT MAUSOLEUM BEAUTIFULLY CRAFTED AROUND 2700 BC.

Hoy where a pair of square chambers is hollowed out of a solid rock outcrop, and an extraordinary 24-seater tomb at Mid Howe on the Isle of Rousay, which is known as the 'Ship of Death'.

The power of the Stones of Stenness and the Ring of Brodgar, neighbouring circles of standing stone circles on Mainland, comes clearly across the ages, but their meaning is unfathomable. More immediate are the dwellings of our distant ancestors. Skara Brae is a village buried in a sand dune whose 4000-year-old houses have been perfectly preserved with their stone tables, beds and shelves. You'll rarely have this celebrated site to yourself. But it's different out on the remote island of Papa Westray, where two houses still stand side by side on the shore at Knap of Howar where they were built some 5500 years ago. On a quiet evening with no one else around, it feels as if the owners have just stepped out to catch a fish or fetch some driftwood, and may at any moment walk through the door and find you there.

IT'S EASY TO UNDERSTAND THE PURPOSE OF ORKNEY'S ANCIENT BURIAL MOUNDS AND STONE-BUILT HOUSES; FAR HARDER TO FATHOM THE REASONS THAT DROVE OUR ANCESTORS TO ERECT GREAT CIRCLES OF SHAPED STONES, SUCH AS THE STONES OF STENNESS ON ORKNEY MAINLAND.

AT SKARA BRAE YOU CAN WALK THE GRASSY DUNE PATHS AND LOOK DOWN INTO THE STONE HOUSES AND ALLEYWAYS OF A VILLAGE BUILT BY ORCADIAN FARMERS AND FISHERS OVER 5000 YEARS AGO.

THE 5500-YEAR-OLD HOUSE AT KNAP OF HOWAR, THE OLDEST DWELLING IN NORTH-WEST EUROPE, STANDS ON THE TINY ISLAND OF PAPA WESTRAY IN A REMOTE CORNER OF THE ORKNEY ARCHIPELAGO.

The Work and the Wars

THE SHETLAND ISLES TO THE SCOTTISH BORDER

The craggy east coast of Scotland is cut by the North Sea to form two tremendous doglegs – the northern tip that slants south-west to Inverness in the crook of the Moray Firth, and then the thick triangular wedge of country that angles down to the twin firths of Tay and Forth and to Edinburgh. There the coastline softens, geometrically if not geologically, as it curves east and south for its final run down to the border with England. Work and wars have shaped the history and the character of this part of the British coast so profoundly that they seem as much part of its foundations as the rocks themselves.

The fish stocks of the North Sea are perilously low, and these days the fishing communities of the far north-east, such as Lybster, Helmsdale and Brora struggle in the face of conservation legislation to carry on with their traditional work. They are having to reinvent themselves as heritage centres, setting out their stalls to attract visitors. Nowhere on this Moray coast, of course, can rival the pulling power of the nondescript village of John O'Groats – which isn't even, as the souvenir-sellers would like you to think, the most northerly point of mainland Britain. If you want to stand on the absolute apex of what travel writer John Hillaby called 'Outermost Gaeldom', you'll need to proceed a couple of miles east of John O'Groats to Duncansby Head, the furthest point from Land's End (876 miles), or travel 15 miles west to go out to Dunnet Head, the northernmost point of land. John O'Groats is the most northerly village, though, and this is where you get your photo taken next to the signpost that says how many miles it is from here to your home town. These photos and the plethora of souvenir shops and B&B places around the village represent serious tourism, the most potent dream for the economic future of this bleak region.

THE LIGHTHOUSE AT THE END OF LYBSTER HARBOUR, BUILT IN 1884 AND SHOWING A RED LIGHT TO DISTINGUISH IT FROM NEIGHBOURING LIGHTHOUSES, LOOKS OUT OVER THE WIDE WATERS OF THE MORAY FIRTH.

THE FAMOUS ADJUSTABLE SIGNPOST AT JOHN O'GROATS – NOT QUITE THE NORTHERNMOST TIP OF MAINLAND BRITAIN, BUT GOOD ENOUGH FOR THE TOURIST TRADE.

MARKING THE TRUE RIM OF 'OUTERMOST GAELDOM' ARE THE DARK CLIFFS OF DUNCANSBY HEAD, AND OUT IN THE BAY A ROW OF TREMENDOUS ROCK STACKS POINTED LIKE TURKISH HATS.

The remote parts of Britain's Celtic fringe have thrown up many a champion of freedom ready to defy the powers that be: William Wallace and Robert the Bruce of Scotland, for example, and Owain Glyndwr of Wales. The north-east Highlands have seen plenty of defiant action, too, both political and personal. It was on Drummossie Moor, just inland of the Moray Firth near Inverness, that the clans under Bonnie Prince Charlie were finally smashed in 1746 by the soldiers of King George II at the Battle of Culloden. Afterwards the Crown built a giant fort at the mouth of the Moray Firth, enclosing 42 acres of ground inside a great rampart strengthened with bastions. Fort George took 21 years to complete, and was a white elephant even before it was finished in 1769 – the clans had been thoroughly subdued by then, and were incapable of swinging a sword in anger.

DUNNET HEAD LIGHTHOUSE ON ITS RUGGED, WEATHER-BEATEN CLIFFS MARKS THE MOST NORTHERLY POINT OF MAINLAND BRITAIN. NORTH FROM HERE ACROSS THE TIDE-RIPPED PENTLAND FIRTH RISE THE CLIFFS OF HOY IN THE ORKNEY ISLANDS.

9 ■ THE WORK AND THE WARS
John O'Groats – Wick – Inverness – Peterhead –
Aberdeen – Dundee – Edinburgh – Eyemouth

The fort squats on its peninsular site, still in military use as a barracks, a strange and mighty spectacle. Opposite it, across the narrow throat of the Moray Firth stands Chanonry Point, where – local legend insists – in 1660 one Coinneach Odhar Fiosaiche (Pale Kenneth the Seer) was publicly burned in a spiked tar barrel for witchcraft. Lady Seaforth ordered the soothsayer's execution, says the story, after flying into a rage while consulting him. She had wanted to know why her husband had not returned home, and Kenneth had rather tactlessly told her the truth: the Earl was in Paris with a woman better-favoured than the Countess herself. A memorial on the spit commemorates the tale. As to why, if the pale seer really had the second sight, he did not foresee the consequences to himself of his honesty – that's a point no one wants to discuss hereabouts. They love the image of the blunt but honest Scot martyred by the cruel and commanding Countess.

THE GREAT MILITARY COMPLEX OF FORT GEORGE, BUILT AT THE MOUTH OF THE MORAY FIRTH BETWEEN 1748 AND 1769, IS IMPRESSIVE ENOUGH FROM GROUND LEVEL, BUT IT'S THE AERIAL VIEW THAT REVEALS ITS TRUE SCALE AND SYMMETRY OF DESIGN.

SANDEND, NEAR PORTSOY, IS A TYPICAL SMALL MORAY FIRTH FISHING VILLAGE, THE QUIETEST PLACE UNDER THE SUN THESE DAYS – THOUGH IT WAS DIFFERENT WHEN THE BIG RUNS OF HERRING WERE TAKING PLACE 100 YEARS AGO.

Further south along the coast, jobs and spending money have been coming ashore in the form of North Sea gas since 1967, with oil from the same marine fields following in 1975. How long the stocks will last seems to be a matter of guesswork, but one day the pipelines will be empty and the economy of Scotland's east coast will be back to fishing and tourism once more. This coast is fishing territory *par excellence*. Every cove and inlet along the Moray shore seems to hold a harbour with a fleet of inshore boats and medium-sized

WELL-SEASONED SMALL TRAWLERS TIE UP IN BUCKIE HARBOUR; SUCH VESSELS CAN STILL EARN A MODEST LIVING FOR A HARD-WORKING SKIPPER AND FAMILY CREW, BUT QUOTAS AND CONSERVATION RESTRICTIONS MAKE IT EVER HARDER.

trawlers – Lossiemouth, Buckie, Cullen, Portsoy, Macduff. Out towards the southward turn of the coast lie the big fishing harbours of Fraserburgh and Peterhead, with Aberdeen 30 miles south along the coast. In 1999 these three harbours between them landed over 170,000 tonnes of fish, worth over £136 million. By 2003 quotas and other restrictions had reduced the tonnage landed to under 150,000, with a value of around £95 million – still big business, but steadily diminishing.

Deep-sea fishing is in the blood of this coast. From the 1750s onwards, whaling ships would set out from ports such as Peterhead, Dundee and Aberdeen for long and dangerous expeditions to the Arctic. The nineteenth century was the heyday of Scottish whaling. The industry limped on intermittently until the 1950s, but is entirely and permanently closed these days. However, far-flung seas still see fishing trawlers from the east coast. The deep-sea boats based at the big ports are technological marvels, equipped with every kind of up-to-date radar and electronic gadgetry. Some are up to 300 feet long; different beasts altogether from the wooden, clinker-built boats still being turned out to order by small boatyards in harbours such as Buckie and Macduff. On the same small scale is the conversion of fresh haddock into the famous 'smokies' at Arbroath further down the coast. Production still goes on in smoking houses in the traditional quarter at the 'fit o' the toon', where pairs of haddocks are tied to wooden sticks and slow-smoked over a wood fire. These Arbroath smokies are a real old-fashioned teatime treat, as are the oak-smoked kippers produced among the fishing towns along the coast of the East Neuk of Fife between the Firths of Tay and Forth.

A HARBOUR FRONT ABLAZE WITH LIGHTS AND THRONGED WITH BIG BOATS TELLS OF ABERDEEN'S PROSPERITY THROUGH FISHING, SHIP REPAIR, OIL RIG CONSTRUCTION AND MAINTENANCE, AND GENERALLY SUPPLYING THE OIL BUSINESS OUT IN THE NORTH SEA.

9 ■ THE WORK AND THE WARS
John O'Groats – Wick – Inverness – Peterhead – Aberdeen – Dundee – Edinburgh – Eyemouth

9 ■ THE WORK AND THE WARS
John O'Groats – Wick – Inverness – Peterhead –
Aberdeen – Dundee – Edinburgh – Eyemouth

The wars of the region have left their mark in many and varied forms. Stark castle ruins stand along the coast – Dunnottar on its flat-topped crag near Aberdeen, the shattered walls of Tantallon overlooking Bass Rock in the Firth of Forth. Bass is one of several small islands in the Firth; most bear witness to the defence requirements of two twentieth-century World Wars in the shape of concrete gun emplacements, searchlight foundations, storesheds and barracks. The eternal human business of spiritual struggle saw hermits settle on these slips of rock; the hermit of Inchcolm sheltered the storm-bound King Alexander for three days in 1123, and the king showed his gratitude for deliverance from death by building the magnificent abbey that stands there today. But the longest-lasting strife has been between man and the elements. That battle reaped its heaviest recorded toll on 14 October 1881, when 129 men from the south-east coast village of Eyemouth were drowned in a sudden and ferocious storm. The tragedy still marks the village, and is remembered in a very beautiful and moving tapestry embroidered by the women of Eyemouth.

◄ THE SHATTERED WALLS OF THE DOUGLAS CLAN STRONGHOLD OF TANTALLON CASTLE LOOK OUT FROM THEIR NORTH BERWICKSHIRE CLIFFS TO THE GREAT BASALT PLUG OF BASS ROCK RISING FROM THE WATERS OF THE FIRTH OF FORTH.

➤ A STRIKING VIEW OF BASS ROCK, HOME TO SOME HUNDRED THOUSAND GANNETS. TO LAND ON BASS AND SPEND A FEW HOURS AMONG SO MANY LARGE, VOCIFEROUS SEABIRDS IS AN OVERWHELMING EXPERIENCE.

The Bleak, the Black and the Beautiful

THE SCOTTISH BORDER TO THE NORTH YORKSHIRE COAST

In all the 3500 miles of the English coastline, the 120-mile stretch between the Scottish border and the cliffs of North Yorkshire is the least well known and the least visited. The northern half, the coastline of Northumberland, has the reputation of being far too bleak, too cold and windswept, to be tempting; while everyone knows that from Newcastle to Hartlepool the coast has been utterly blackened and ruined by shipbuilding and coal mining.

As with most rumours, there's a grain of truth in this ugly porridge of a picture. It's certainly true that the Northumbrian coast can be bleak and windy, and that if you crave an ice-cream van and an amusement arcade every couple of miles it probably isn't for you. But there is so much beauty in the mile upon mile of empty sandy beaches, the flowery dunes, the islands rising offshore and the great castles frowning from their crags over lonely strands and green breakers, that if the sea were only a few degrees warmer and the wind a touch less bracing, these sands would be as crowded as Blackpool Beach. Thank your lucky stars they are not. As for the poisoned shore around Wearmouth and the Durham coast – that's the way it used to be

in the North-East's harsh and vibrant era of heavy industry. But those days are gone. Beauty has crept in unheralded. Nature, with a little help from man, is cleaning those grimy cliffs and beaches and re-clothing those rubbish-choked stream valleys in green. This is a fabulous success story,

BLAST BEACH BELOW DAWDON COLLIERY BEFORE THE PIT'S CLOSURE IN 1991; NOTE THE THICK SCAB OF COLLIERY SPOIL AND WASTE THAT LOCALS CHRISTENED 'MINESTONE'.

WILD FLOWERS GRACE THE MAGNESIAN LIMESTONE CLIFFTOPS AT BEACON POINT NEAR EASINGTON COLLIERY, ONCE A BYWORD FOR POLLUTION AND INDUSTRIAL FILTH.

the rediscovery of a whole coastline that everyone had forgotten was there.

As with so much of the British coastline, the history of the Northumbrian coast is intimately bound up with strife. This was all border country throughout the troubled Middle Ages. Scots and English armies attacked and retreated, besieged and resisted, captured and yielded, slaughtered and died in a deadly dance of war that lasted many hundreds of years. When the two nations' forces weren't contesting the ground with each other, it was the turn of local warlords and opportunists, cattle thieves and wild rogues to make things hot for the inhabitants of this lawless no-man's-land of a region. No wonder immense strongholds such as Bamburgh, Dunstanburgh and Warkworth were founded on the coast, castles of the mighty that still frown threateningly over the empty landscape and the bare islands that rise offshore.

A volcanic intrusion of black dolerite rock known as the Whin Sill crosses much of the north of England, ultimately surfacing around Bamburgh before plunging into the North

OF ALL NORTHUMBERLAND'S COASTAL STRONGHOLDS, BAMBURGH CASTLE IS THE MOST IMPRESSIVE, PERCHING ON A GREAT CRAG OF THE WHIN SILL AND LOOKING OUT OVER PEERLESS WHITE SANDS TO THE FARNE ISLANDS.

Sea. Bamburgh Castle, perched on this last land outcrop, stares out at the final manifestation of the Whin Sill – the seal-haunted archipelago of rocky platforms that form the Farne Islands. These and their neighbouring 'big sister' island of Holy Island (or Lindisfarne) were the settings for struggle, too: the combat between early Christian hermits and the world, the flesh and the Devil. St Cuthbert, the shy seventh-century shepherd boy who became a reluctant bishop, lived on Holy Island and then on Inner Farne in great frugality and discomfort, fighting cowled demons riding on goats that he certainly took to be very real and deadly adversaries. The monks who followed St Cuthbert

THE POLYGONAL KEEP OF WARKWORTH CASTLE, BUILT IN THE FOURTEENTH CENTURY DURING THE TURBULENT BORDER WARS, NOWADAYS GUARDS A TRANQUIL BEND IN THE UPPER ESTUARY OF THE RIVER COQUET.

PERFECTLY SET LIKE A 1930s RAILWAY ADVERTISEMENT, THE SPECTACULAR RUINS OF DUNSTANBURGH CASTLE RISE BEYOND THE STREAKY YELLOW AND PURPLE SANDS OF EMBLETON BAY.

10 ■ THE BLEAK, THE BLACK AND THE BEAUTIFUL
Berwick-upon-Tweed – Holy Island – Bamburgh – Amble –
Newcastle-upon-Tyne – Sunderland – Hartlepool

on Lindisfarne also had to battle with inner demons, with poverty and isolation; yet they found the inspiration to create one of the world's most beautiful illuminated manuscripts, the Farne Gospels. The most famous Farne Island battle of all was the one waged on the wild morning of 7 September 1838 by a slender woman of 23 as she tried to snatch a group of terrified shipwreck victims from the grasp of a North Sea storm. Grace Darling and her father William, the Longstone lighthouse keeper, could only save 9 out of 52 souls from the paddle steamer *Forfarshire*, but the selfless bravery

GREY SEALS OF THE FARNE ISLANDS HAUL THEMSELVES OUT OF THE WATER TO BASK IN THE LEE OF THE LONGSTONE LIGHTHOUSE, FROM WHICH GRACE AND HER FATHER WILLIAM DARLING ROWED OUT ON THEIR EPIC RESCUE VENTURE ON 7 SEPTEMBER 1838.

10 ■ THE BLEAK, THE BLACK AND THE BEAUTIFUL
Berwick-upon-Tweed – Holy Island – Bamburgh – Amble – Newcastle-upon-Tyne – Sunderland – Hartlepool

EDWARD HUDSON,
FOUNDER OF *COUNTRY
LIFE*, EMPLOYED THE TOP
DESIGNERS OF THE DAY
WHEN HE HAD THE TUDOR
FORTRESS OF LINDISFARNE
CASTLE CONVERTED INTO
A COUNTRY HOUSE IN THE
1900s – SIR EDWIN LUTYENS
WAS THE ARCHITECT, WHILE
GERTRUDE JEKYLL LAID OUT
THE WALLED GARDEN.

of the pair – and the youth and beauty of
Grace – made them national heroes.

The Northumbrian coast has its black legacy,
the old coal port of Amble where colliery
wagons from the pits north of Newcastle-
upon-Tyne would bring the 'black diamond'

for loading into sailing colliers destined for all
the ports of England. Some of the old staithes
or coal jetties can still be seen here, but that's
the extent of the visible coal-mining heritage.
North from Amble stretch the glorious
beaches: Alnmouth Bay, Boulmer Haven,
Embleton and Beadnell Bays, Seahouses and

Bamburgh Sands, Budle Bay and Goswick Sands. To anyone who has walked or cycled this coast, or ridden a horse for miles through the surf, or come to the beaches with a sailboard or a pair of birdwatching binoculars or a toddler with good circulation and plenty of energy to burn, these names ring like a eulogy. It's impossible to deny that the sea can be so cold in high summer that it will make an unwary swimmer scream at first plunge, or that you need your coat collar turned up most days of the year. But here on these windy beaches and flower-spattered cliffs, you'll find a double dose of pure, sheer exhilaration.

The great shipbuilding rivers of Tyne and Wear wind through their respective cities of Newcastle and Sunderland and reach the sea only eight miles apart. Ships are still made in small numbers at the Swan Hunter yard on Tyneside, but the Wear flows quiet and clean through Sunderland these days. It is the coastline to the south of Wearmouth, though, that carries the big surprise for anyone who knew it in the old days but has not seen it since the last of County Durham's clifftop coal mines closed down.

THE RIVER ALN CURVES TO MEET THE SEA
THROUGH MIGHTY SANDBANKS, AS SHOWN IN
THIS SUPERB AERIAL SHOT OF THE ALN ESTUARY
CRADLING ALNMOUTH ON ITS
LOW-LYING PROMONTORY.

CHANGEABLE WEATHER: THE NORTH SEA SENDS FREQUENT STORMS CHARGING ACROSS THE NORTHUMBRIAN COAST, BUT THESE ARE USUALLY CHASED INLAND BY BELTS OF BEAUTIFUL SUNNY WEATHER THAT MAKE THE SANDS GLOW AND THE COLD SEA SPARKLE.

10 ■ THE BLEAK, THE BLACK AND THE BEAUTIFUL
Berwick-upon-Tweed – Holy Island – Bamburgh – Amble –
Newcastle-upon-Tyne – Sunderland – Hartlepool

ONE OF THE MANY REMARKABLE FEATURES OF THE NORTHUMBRIAN COAST IS THE EXTENSIVE RANGE OF SAND DUNES THAT BACKS IT. HERE THE DUNES OF BUDLE BAY GLOW IN THE UNEARTHLY, SULPHUROUS LIGHT OF EVENING.

This was the place made famous in the 1971 film *Get Carter*, in which Michael Caine chases and is chased by gangsters through a hellish industrial moonscape of colliery tips, filthy beaches and sinister cableways of clanking iron waste buckets. The coal pits of the East Durham coastline were opened only in the 1900s, but during the few decades that followed, the beaches and sea became indescribably foul with waste and coal sludge dumped from the mines and with raw sewage deposited by the pit villages. No one in those days could have visualized this blasted and blighted coastline as a visitor destination where walkers and wildlife enthusiasts would flock, nor as an area so rich in plant and bird life that it could be worthy of designation as an SSSI (Site of Special Scientific Interest), let along a Heritage Coast and an SAC (Special Area of Conservation). Yet such has been the energy put into 'Turning the Tide', the plan to restore the region after the last collieries closed in 1993, that those unlikely things have come to pass. It's a small form of modern miracle: 12 miles of beautiful coast brought back from the dead.

Beyond Hartlepool the land rises gradually to form the splendid cliffs of the North Yorkshire coastline. The bleakness here comes from the occasional North Sea fog, the blackness from the jet that was mined from the cliffs and shaped into the strings of highly polished beads so beloved of the Victorians. The beauty, as everywhere along this connoisseur's coast, remains in the eye of the beholder.

Cliffs and Crumbles

THE NORTH YORKSHIRE COAST TO THE WASH

If ever there was a coastline of two halves, this is it – although if you are counting off the miles, there is about four times as much crumbling or dead flat shore between the North Yorkshire coast and the mighty estuary of the Wash as there are ramparts of cliffs. Through the ferocity of winter storms and the gentle persuasion of lapping tides, the North Sea is steadily diminishing this coast, slyly pilfering a foot or two of marshland here, grabbing a chunk of cliff by assault and battery there. Geology decides what stays and what goes: the hard Jurassic limestone of the Scarborough promontory defying the waves, the soft black clay of the Holderness cliffs yielding yards of ground each winter to the sea. It is a coastline that's constantly changing, either eroding or building, forever on the move – and almost always inland.

The 'Dinosaur Coast' runs south for 35 miles from the fishing village of Staithes on the Yorkshire/Cleveland border to the promontory of Filey Brigg, a nose of hard limestone full of shells and sands. Dinosaur footprints have been discovered in the sandstone of the cliffs at Whitby, the remains of prehistoric fish-lizards and crocodiles in the limestone and mudstone of the cliffs

IT'S NOT ONLY THE SOFT CLAY CLIFFS OF SOUTHERN YORKSHIRE AND LINCOLNSHIRE THAT ARE BEING ATTACKED BY THE SEA; TO THE NORTH THE CALCAREOUS GRITS OF FILEY BRIGG'S LONG HEADLAND ARE ERODING YEAR BY YEAR.

A NARROW INLET IN THE NORTH YORKSHIRE CLIFFS SHELTERS THE HIGHLY PICTURESQUE FISHING VILLAGE OF STAITHES, THE PLACE FROM WHICH YOUNG JAMES COOK RAN AWAY TO WHITBY, MARKING THE START OF HIS LIFE-LONG ADVENTURING BY SEA.

LOOKING ALONG THE PEBBLY NORTH YORKSHIRE SHORE FROM THE OLD ALUM WORKS AT STOUPE BROW TOWARDS THE HEADLAND OF RAVENSCAR, PITTED WITH OLD MINERAL WORKINGS AND THICK WITH FOSSILS OF LEAVES, FLOWERS AND FERNS.

11 ■ CLIFFS AND CRUMBLES
Whitby – Robin Hood's Bay – Scarborough – Filey –
Bridlington – Hornsea – Spurn Head – Skegness

THE MAGNIFICENT CLIFFS OF FLAMBOROUGH HEAD ARE RIDDLED WITH CRACKS AND CAVES
BURROWED OUT OF THE CHALK BY THE SEA. UNDERWATER FORMATIONS MAKE THE TIDES AROUND
THE HEAD PARTICULARLY TRICKY; ONLY LOCALS REALLY KNOW HOW TO NEGOTIATE THEM.

WHITBY LIFEBOAT STATION, ONE OF SIX ALONG JUST 50 MILES OF TREACHEROUS COAST, IS ONE OF THE
LONGEST-SERVING – IT WAS ESTABLISHED IN 1802. WHITBY HAS BEEN AN INSHORE STATION SINCE 1966,
AND HER CREWS HAVE SO FAR BEEN AWARDED 35 RNLI MEDALS, INCLUDING FIVE GOLD.

between here and Robin Hood's Bay.
Sand and mud spread by river deltas some
160 million years ago solidified to form the
tall cliffs at Ravenscar, and here you can see
the fossil prints of the leaves, flowers and
ferns of that ancient world. There are corals
in the cliffs near Filey Brigg, and great walls
of wave-burrowed chalk at Bempton and
Flamborough Head that were laid down in
seas warmer than those that wash these cliffs
today. And when the world turned colder
and the long cycle of ice ages began, their
mark was left here too, in the shape of big
boulders dragged in the skirts of the melting
glaciers and dumped on the Yorkshire shore
where they still lie.

Life along the cliffs has always been a tough
affair. Fishermen still use the same design of
coble or fishing boat that their Scandinavian
ancestors developed, the sharply pointed
prow and stern allowing the boat to be
launched and manoeuvred forwards or
backwards in seas that are often rough,
always tricky with currents. There are six
lifeboats stationed along the 50 miles of coast
between Staithes and Bridlington, and they
are all kept busy. In times past, smuggling
was a way of life, especially in the impossibly
picturesque fishing village of Robin Hood's
Bay, which tumbles in a red-roofed huddle
down a cleft in the cliffs between Whitby
and Scarborough.

MAGNIFICENT NINETEENTH-CENTURY SEASIDE ARCHITECTURE
AT SCARBOROUGH, WHOSE LONG SOUTH BAY BEACH SWEEPS
ROUND UNDER THE LIMESTONE RIDGE OF CASTLE HEADLAND
AND THE REMNANTS OF THE TWELFTH-CENTURY CASTLE WALLS.

11 ■ CLIFFS AND CRUMBLES
Whitby – Robin Hood's Bay – Scarborough – Filey –
Bridlington – Hornsea – Spurn Head – Skegness

It was a great boost to the local economy when the seaside holiday boom got properly underway with the coming of the railways in the mid-nineteenth century. Suddenly the genteel classes were venturing in numbers to roost among the fisherfolk of Staithes and Robin Hood's Bay, while whole towns from the industrial heart of Yorkshire would decamp en masse during the Wakes Week (summer) holidays to the boarding houses and beaches of Scarborough and Bridlington. But this exposure to the outside world never quite smoothed away the quirks and oddities of the 'funny folk' of the coast. Flamborough fishermen had their own sword dance, which they didn't really like outsiders to penetrate. The fishermen of nineteenth-century Filey were known to be a godless lot of foul-mouthed boozers, prone to chasing evangelists out of town with a volley of dried skate – until they were all converted by 'Praying Johnny' Oxtoby, became model Methodist lay preachers, and started their own fervent Fishermen's Choir. Not that all Christian singing along the Yorkshire coast was joyful. At funerals the women would keen a special dirge that was remarkable for its mournfulness:

This yah neet, this yah neet,
Ivvery neet an' all,
Fire an' fleet an' cannul leet,
An' Christ tak up thi saul.

When thoo frae hence away art passed
Ivvery neet an' all,
Ti Whinny Moor thoo cums at last,
An' Christ tak up thi saul.

MORE TREMENDOUS SEASIDE BUILDINGS ABOVE NORTH BEACH AT BRIDLINGTON. VICTORIAN RESORT ARCHITECTS PLANNED FOR GRANDEUR; FOR MOST HOLIDAYMAKERS, THE ANNUAL WEEK BY THE SEA WAS THEIR ONE CHANCE TO BRUSH SHOULDERS WITH GLAMOUR AND FANTASY.

Turning south from Flamborough Head and Bridlington, it's as if you enter an entirely different world. The cliffs shrink to stumpy ledges a few feet high, a platform of dark crumbly clay laid down by the retreating glaciers. The North Sea is eating these shaky cliffs as a hungry child eats sponge cake. Abandoned houses and broken caravan parks perch precariously on the edge of the cliffs, almost suspended in mid-air, above the sands of Barmston, Ulrome and Skipsea.

The sea is making its way inland at a rate of dozens of feet each year, and there's nothing at all to be done about it. The flattened tableland of Holderness stretches from Bridlington to Spurn Head in one unbroken line, 40 miles long and 15 broad, with hardly a contour line to disturb the level horizon; a very slightly concave seaboard with only one first-class road and the two half-forgotten resorts of Hornsea and Withernsea. A coast that's not for jet-setting fun seekers, but for those who appreciate the triste pleasures of a moody, lonely shore.

THE EAST YORKSHIRE RESORT OF HORNSEA LIES AMONG FAST-CRUMBLING CLAY CLIFFS ON A COAST THAT FORMS ONE TREMENDOUS, UNBROKEN LINE SOME 40 MILES LONG – ONE OF BRITAIN'S GREATEST BEACHES, REMARKABLY UNFREQUENTED AND UNSPOILED.

11 ■ CLIFFS AND CRUMBLES
Whitby – Robin Hood's Bay – Scarborough – Filey –
Bridlington – Hornsea – Spurn Head – Skegness

The curving anteater snout of the Spurn Head promontory forms the upper jaw of the great mouth of the River Humber, five miles wide where it surges seaward as the boundary between Yorkshire and Lincolnshire. The Humber Estuary is one of Britain's prime birdwatching sites, though you need to be in a boat with a good pair of binoculars to get the most out of the gulls and waders that throng the vast sandbanks. A boat would get you up close to the strange, evocative hulk of Bull Sand Fort, a block-like concrete stronghold built into the estuary during the First World War to safeguard coastal convoys as they assembled at the mouth of the Humber. From here the coast of Lincolnshire trends away south in an enormous seaward bulge. If Holderness is flat, Lincolnshire's coastal districts of East Lindsey and South Holland are contourless pancakes. Their 70-mile shore slips seamlessly into the North Sea through marsh, sands and mud flats. The giant three-sided estuary of The Wash melds with the sea in a maze of creeks and deeps, muds and sandbanks. Only the long sea walls and the built-up bits of coast around the resorts of Mablethorpe and Skegness prevent the sea charging inland at high tide and repossessing the land that men reclaimed from it, land that formed its bed not long ago.

The ancient people of this coast learned to fear the tidal wave or 'aegre' that would occasionally rise and devastate their country. In the terrible East Coast flood disaster of 31 January 1953, 43 people were drowned when the sea overwhelmed the coast between Mablethorpe and Skegness. With rising sea levels and changing attitudes to the viability of hard sea defences, the future of the Lincolnshire coast will be one of 'managed retreat' – an adjustment and a compromise between the tenacity of man and the blind hunger of the sea.

DEAR OLD SKEGGY – THE SANDS AT SKEGNESS ARE BEAUTIFUL
AND UNCROWDED AT MOST TIMES OF THE YEAR, BUT 'BRACING'
ENOUGH IN THEIR EXPOSURE TO THE BRISK NORTH SEA WEATHER
TO MAKE A WINDBREAK A PRACTICAL NECESSITY.

The Fracturing Coast

THE WASH TO THE THAMES ESTUARY

It was a winter storm in the New Year of 1999 that stripped the final
layer of peat from the ancient buried saltmarsh on Holne Beach.
There, exposed to the North Norfolk skies, lay Seahenge, a circle of
55 stumpy timbers planted in the sands some 4000 years ago. At the
hub of the circle the builders of Seahenge had inverted a great oak
tree trunk and driven it headfirst into the marsh so that its roots
stood exposed, cradling a flat surface like a table or an altar.

Who knows how many times over the four millennia of Seahenge's
existence the sea has abruptly offered the monument to men's
gaze, and as suddenly concealed it again? Now, at the turn of the
twenty-first century, using state-of-the-art technology and know-how,
archaeologists have salvaged the crumbling old timbers from their
remote tidal bed and taken them away to be preserved for posterity.
But many condemned this as an act of desecration. Druids, tree-
worshippers, poets, naturalists, lovers of the bleak foreshore of
the immense Wash estuary – they saw the shifting, mysterious
monument, given or withdrawn in an unpredictable cycle at the
whim of tide and weather, as representing the very spirit of this
ever-changing East Anglian coastline.

A great elongated semi-circle of coast runs for 150 miles by way of
Norfolk through Suffolk and on down into Essex, from the eastern
flank of The Wash to the mouth of the Thames. Most of it is crumbling
and tottering, slumping or sliding into the sea. The North Sea tides
never rest, felling cliffs and sucking away dunes, always eating into
the land, always hungry to claim back rich arable fields and built-upon
acres that once lay under the sea and will do so again one day –
perhaps sooner than we think, if global warming causes sea levels

TWO BLACK LOGS LIE IN A POOL ON THE NORTH NORFOLK
FORESHORE NEAR HOLME-NEXT-THE-SEA – NOT THE MOST
VISUALLY EXCITING OF ARCHAEOLOGICAL SITES, BUT THIS PAIR
OF TIMBERS FORMS PART OF THE GREAT WOODEN HENGE OR
WORSHIP SITE OF SEAHENGE, BUILT SOME 4000 YEARS AGO
AND EXPOSED BY THE TIDE IN 1999.

A GEOLOGICAL LAYER-CAKE FORMS THE STRIPED CLIFFS AT
HUNSTANTON – A CHOCOLATE-BROWN LAYER OF IRON-RICH
SANDSTONE AT BEACH LEVEL, THEN A BAND OF HUNSTANTON
RED CHALK, TOPPED WITH A BLANKET OF WHITE CHALK.

to continue to rise. The red and white striped cliffs at Hunstanton, the yellow ones at Cromer and the brown cliffs of Happisburgh are all falling to wave erosion at varying rates, while breaches in the shingle bank at Aldeburgh in Suffolk threaten the little town where Benjamin Britten lived and composed his sea-inspired music. Just along the stony coast, the clifftops at Dunwich hold a single fragment of a medieval Franciscan monastery; all the other buildings, the nine churches and marketplace and splendid walls of the ancient capital of East Anglia, have been swallowed by the sea over the centuries. Further south, in Essex, landowners are already allowing the sea to come through man-made defences and flood selected areas.

Not that the North Sea always does its work so subtly and gradually. On the terrible night of 31 January 1953, a wind-assisted sea surge battered Britain's eastern coast so ferociously that more than 300 people died. Fifty-eight of them were in little Canvey Island on the Essex shore of the River Thames, lying below sea level and guarded by inadequate sea walls.

THE SUFFOLK COASTAL TOWN OF ALDEBURGH IS AN UPMARKET RESORT WITH FEW ROWDY SEASIDE AMENITIES, BUT PLENTY OF SHINGLE AND FRESH AIR, AND THE BEST FISH AND CHIPS IN EAST ANGLIA.

ON A LOVELY CALM DAY THE NORTH SEA TIDE SMASHES INTO THE SEA DEFENCES AT HAPPISBURGH; IN STORM CONDITIONS THE POWER OF THESE SEAS IS A GENUINE THREAT TO THE CRUMBLING EAST NORFOLK COAST.

In some places, though, the sea is retreating
from the land. All along the North Norfolk
coast stand little red-roofed and flint-walled
ports – Stiffkey, Morston, Wiveton, Cley,
Salthouse – marooned a mile or so inland.
Their magnificent churches bear witness
to the prosperity that the sea brought them
through coastal trade in medieval times. Now
they lie quiet in retirement as holiday havens,
cut off from the North Sea by vast swathes of
marshland that have grown on the rich silt
of coastal rivers. And hereabouts the sea can
be a builder, too. Spits and islands of shingle
such as Blakeney Point and Scolt Head Island
in Norfolk, and the mighty ten-mile-long
shingle bank of Orford Ness that forms the
bent elbow of the Suffolk coast, continue
to grow offshore, little by little, as the sea
drags and mounds the unending supply
of flint pebbles that roll in their tens of
millions up and down this dynamic,
always changing shore.

A GATEWAY AND A FEW
FRAGMENTS OF WALL ARE
ALL THAT REMAINS OF THE
FRANCISCAN MONASTERY
AT DUNWICH; THE REST
OF THE MEDIEVAL TOWN,
CHIEF PORT OF EAST
ANGLIA, HAS BEEN
SWALLOWED UP BY
THE SEA.

WITH ITS OPEN, FLAT LANDSCAPE AND STRONG SEA WINDS, THE NORTH NORFOLK
COAST IS IDEAL FOR WINDMILLS, AND THE EIGHTEENTH-CENTURY TOWER MILL AT
CLEY-NEXT-THE-SEA IS ONE OF THE DISTRICT'S BEST-KNOWN LANDMARKS.

A BRISK BREEZE AND A FINE DAY ENTICE HUNDREDS OF BOATERS TO EXPLORE THE
DUNES AND CREEKS AROUND THE COAST OF NORTH NORFOLK – BIRTHPLACE OF
ADMIRAL LORD NELSON AND MANY OTHER FAMOUS SAILORS.

Down the centuries the trading and seafaring settlements of the East Anglian coast have lost out to the sea's remorseless demolition and barrier-building. Yet seabirds and wildfowl have never had it so good. Norfolk's coastal marshes and reed beds teem with waders and songbirds in spring and summer. In the winter it is the turn of the pinkfoot, greylag and brent geese, the aerial clouds of wigeon, pintail and teal, and other wildfowl arriving for the cold months to congregate and feed on the inland fields and the coastal mud flats as General Winter marches across their Siberian and Arctic homelands.

Further south stretch the great Suffolk coast heathlands, broad areas of heather, scrub and pine forest. They play host to marsh and hen harriers, owls, peregrine and sparrowhawk; while in summer the blue-legged avocets, delicate black and white waders with upturned bills, breed around Havergate Island in the estuary of the River Ore. As for the moody, muddy banks, creeks and islets of the unfrequented Essex coast – their very essence seems caught in winter when crowds of dark-bellied brent geese pass across a lemon-yellow dawn, gabbling and yelping like great packs of spectral sky hounds.

VAST NUMBERS OF WADING BIRDS CONGREGATE TO FEED ON THE MUD FLATS OF THE WASH ESTUARY. KNOT IS ONE OF THE SPECIES THAT FORM FLOCKS SEVERAL THOUSAND STRONG, A SPECTACULAR SIGHT AS THE INCOMING TIDE CONCENTRATES THEM IN A TIGHTLY PACKED MASS.

12 ■ THE FRACTURING COAST
Wells-next-the-Sea – Cromer – Happisburgh – Great Yarmouth – Southwold – Aldeburgh – Clacton-on-Sea – Canvey Island

In the end it is this moodiness, a bleak and elemental atmosphere, that best summarizes the fracturing coast of East Anglia. People of strong character with a penchant for such places and a desire to get away from it all find their niches in reed-roofed Norfolk huts, in Suffolk marshmen's cottages and on home-built houseboats moored up in the muddy Essex creeks and tidal streams. Out at Paglesham Churchend, on the remotest corner of the River Roach, once lived a famous eighteenth-century smuggler named Hard Apple, who would wrestle bulls, drink whole kegs of rum and eat broken glass for fun. A man like that was made for this rugged, back-of-beyond coast that juts with such defiance into the always oncoming North Sea.

WELLS-NEXT-THE-SEA STILL MAKES A LIVING FROM COASTAL TRADE, THANKS TO ITS CHANNEL THAT CUTS THROUGH THE MARSHES TO THE SEA. BUT THESE DAYS MOST PROSPERITY COMES FROM SECOND-HOMERS AND HOLIDAYMAKERS, WHOSE BEACH HUTS DOT THE DUNES A MILE OR MORE SEAWARD OF THE OLD PORT.

A YOUNG GREYLAG GOOSE SKITTERS OVER THE WATER; THESE LARGE PALE GEESE WITH THE YELLOW-ORANGE BILL ARE FREQUENT VISITORS TO EAST ANGLIA IN WINTER, WITH SOME STAYING ON ALL YEAR ROUND.

GAZETTEER

SYMBOLS AND ABBREVIATIONS

✆ Contact telephone number

🚗 Directions by road

🚢 Ferry information

✈ Air travel information

AONB Area of Outstanding Natural Beauty

CADW The Welsh equivalent of English Heritage – cadw is Welsh for 'to keep'

EH English Heritage

EHS Environmental and Heritage Service

EN English Nature

HS Heritage Scotland

LNR Local Nature Reserve

NNR National Nature Reserve

NT National Trust (**NTS/NTNI** National Trust Scotland/Northern Ireland)

RAMSAR Stands for 'a wetland included in the Ramsar List of Wetlands of International Importance' – this agreement was signed in Ramsar, a town in Iran.

RSPB Royal Society for the Protection of Birds

SAC Special Area of Conservation

SNH Scottish Natural Heritage

TIC Tourist Information Centre

UNESCO United Nations Educational, Scientific and Cultural Organization

WWT The Wildfowl & Wetlands Trust

Introduction

This Gazetteer lists and describes treasures of the British coast featured in the BBC 2 series *Coast*, along with thousands of other sites along the coast. It offers a host of practical ideas for enjoying this priceless national heritage to the full.

Each of the 12 sections is dedicated to the territory explored in one of the earlier chapters and also in the accompanying TV series. Under a range of headings you'll find suggestions pointing you towards activities such as birdwatching, fishing, sailing, walking; natural features from cliffs, beaches and sand dunes to estuaries, lagoons and marshes; islands and coastal castles; seaside resorts and other places of interest all around our shores. Road and ferry directions, telephone numbers and websites will help you plan your visit.

Entrance fees, opening times and facilities on offer can change from season to season and year to year, so it's always a good idea to phone particular places or check on their websites for this sort of information before you set out.

At the end of each section you'll find a list of useful websites, including those for the most important organizations looking after the coast and its buildings, historic sites, natural environment and wildlife. The websites have huge amounts of information on specific locations, guided tours, special offers, children's activities and so on.

Winchester

M3

HAMP

Southampton

A31

The Solent

Cowes

M27

DEVON

M5

A35

Newport

DORSET

Poole

Bournemouth

Isle of Wight

Exeter

Lyme Regis

A35

Hurst
Castle

Beer

Poole
Bay

The Needles

A La Ronde

Abbotsbury

Lyme Bay

Isle of
Purbeck

Studland
Bay

Exmouth

Weymouth

Swanage

Exe
Estuary

Chesil Beach

Weymouth
Bay

Durdle
Door

Dawlish Warren

Portland Bill

Isle of
Portland

St. Catherine's
Point

0   10   20 kilometres

0   10   20 miles

The Straits of Dover to the Exe Estuary

THE DEFIANT COAST

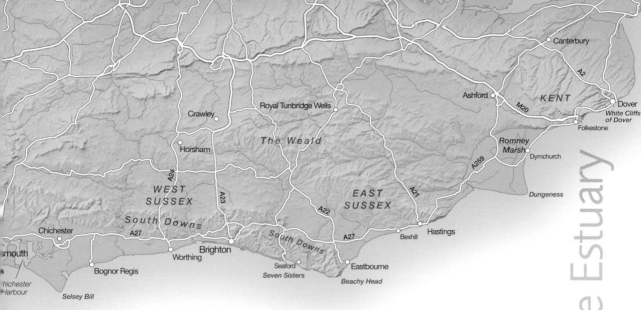

ACTIVITIES

■ Sailing

The Isle of Wight is one of Britain's prime centres for small-boat sailing, and the time to be there is during Cowes Week (generally the first week in August), when hundreds of boats from tiny dinghies to big ocean-going yachts compete in races or just sail around and bask in reflected glory.

▶ *Cowes TIC* ✆ *01983 813818;* **www.cowes.co.uk**

■ Fossil hunting

Fossil hunting is wonderful along the Jurassic Coast (see **Places of Interest** on page 133), especially at the feet of the crumbling cliffs around Lyme Regis: Golden Cap, Stonebarrow and Black Ven to the east, Ware Cleeves to the west.

■ Birdwatching

You'll find excellent birdwatching on Dungeness, Kent (sea birds and birds of passage), Arne RSPB Reserve on Poole Harbour (nightjar, Dartford warbler), the Fleet Lagoon behind Chesil Beach (wading birds, swans) and Chesil Beach itself (tern, ringed plover, skylark – NB restrictions in breeding season, March–July).

ISLANDS

■ Isle of Wight

The diamond-shaped Isle of Wight, across the Solent channel from Southampton, measures only 23 miles from east to west and 13 from north to south. Packed into this small space are great cliffs and fossil beaches, farmlands and woods, villages and towns, river valleys and steep ravines, all joined by a superb 500-mile network of footpaths.

🚢 *From Southampton to Cowes, or from Lymington to Yarmouth*

▶ *Isle of Wight TIC* ✆ *01983 813818*

■ Isle of Portland

The Isle of Portland is connected to the mainland south of Weymouth by a narrow neck of land. Portland has been quarried for building stone for 600 years; its hard-wearing but easily worked limestone was used by Sir Christopher Wren for the rebuilding of London after the Great Fire of 1666. With its bare quarry ledges and brace of stark old prisons, Portland can seem a grim place. The isle is best appreciated when bright sunshine brings out the silvery glow of the stone.

🚗 *A354 from Weymouth*

▶ **www.swuklink.com**

NATURAL WORLD

■ Cliffs

CHALK

Tiny organisms called *foraminifera* lived and died in the Great Chalk Sea that covered most of Europe some 100 million years ago. Their remains formed massive deposits on the sea floor. Compressed into a band 1700 feet thick, this layer of *foraminifera* shells is exposed along the Kent and East Sussex coast – for example, in the

splendid White Cliffs of Dover, Beachy Head
(540 feet) and the Seven Sisters (500 feet).
▶ *White Cliffs of Dover Visitor Centre (NT), Upper
Road, Langdon Cliffs, nr Dover* ✆ *01304 202756*
▶ *Beachy Head Countryside Centre, Beachy Head
Road, Beachy Head, Eastbourne, East Sussex*
✆ *01323 737273;* **www.eastbourne.org**

GREENSAND AND BLUE LIAS
Around Lyme Regis, the Dorset coast cliffs are
distinctly shaky. A topping of chalk and greensand sits
unsteadily on a band of blue lias, with a thin, slippery
layer of greasy black gault between them. The clifftops
of Golden Cap and Stonebarrow to the east of Lyme
retain their fresh gold colours, thanks to frequent falls
of the weather-beaten outer layers, and to the west the
cliffs of Ware Cleeves are tumbling gradually – and
sometimes dramatically – to the fossil-strewn beach.
▶ *TIC* ✆ *01297 442138*

LIMESTONE
In the Isle of Purbeck Peninsula at the eastern
end of the 'Jurassic Coast' of Dorset, the exposed
limestone cliffs around Durlstone Head contain
Purbeck/Portland limestone, a very hard stone,
easily quarried, highly durable and much in demand
as building stone. There are spectacular quarry
workings, ledges and caverns at places such as
Winspit and Tilly Whim Caves, though for safety
reasons they are not accessible to the public.

■ **Lagoons**
The great shingle bank of Chesil Beach in Dorset
shelters the shallow, brackish waters of the Fleet
Lagoon, which is warmer in summer and colder in
winter than the surrounding area. Its semi-salty water
supports large varieties of seaweeds, and enough
kinds of molluscs and aquatic plants to feed a large
number of birds species, including the hundreds of
swans resident at the Abbotsbury Swannery.
🚗 *Between Weymouth and Bridport on the
B3157 coastal road*

■ **Natural harbours**
CHICHESTER HARBOUR, WEST SUSSEX
A beautiful inlet that widens from a narrow entrance
opposite East Head into a broad maze of creeks, islets

and peninsulas. Footpaths run round most of the
shoreline; the Chichester Harbour Conservancy has
produced a pack of ten leaflets about walks around
Chichester Harbour.
▶ *Chichester Harbour Conservancy* ✆ *01243 512301*

POOLE HARBOUR, DORSET
Only five miles from east to west and with a
narrow entrance, the inlet of Poole Harbour has
two high tides a day and a shoreline so full of creeks
and bays that it measures more than 100 miles. Red
squirrels thrive on the National Trust's Brownsea
Island, and on the west shore of the harbour are two
outstanding nature reserves – Arne RSPB Reserve for
rare nightjars and Dartford warblers, and Studland
and Godlingston Heath National Nature Reserve
for snakes and lizards.
▶ *NT; RSPB; EN*

■ **Sea stacks**
OLD HARRY AND HIS WIFE, STUDLAND BAY, DORSET
Handfast Point forms the southern arm of Studland
Bay, and in the sea off its tip stands Old Harry, a blocky
chalk stack. The chalk pinnacle of Old Harry's Wife,
out beyond her husband, is fast crumbling.

THE NEEDLES, ISLE OF WIGHT
Three slim blades of chalk rising from the sea at the
sharp western tip of the Isle of Wight, The Needles are
a famous landmark, especially when bright sunlight
makes them shimmer white, or when winter storms
send waves bursting over them.
▶ *The Needles Park (tourist attraction)* ✆ *0870 458 0022*

■ **Shingle**
CHESIL BEACH, DORSET
A giant pebble beach 18 miles long. Rare beach plants
thrive here, as do nesting birds such as terns, ringed
plover and skylark. Beach fishermen love the bank,
too. In days of sail Chesil Beach was notorious
for shipwrecks – one of the worst occurred on
18 November 1795, when over 1000 soldiers and
crew members drowned when three military
transports were driven ashore.
▶ *Chesil Bank and Fleet Nature Reserve, Portland*
✆ *01305 760579;* **www.coastlink.org**
▶ **www.weymouth.here-on-the.net/shipwrecks.html**

DUNGENESS, KENT

Europe's largest vegetated shingle spit, Dungeness is a weird and wonderful place – a vast prairie of pebbles that blooms with rare plants; a dry wasteland thronged with birds where the RSPB maintains a reserve; a place of extreme loneliness where fishermen congregate; an elemental desert over-shadowed by a nuclear power station. Film maker Derek Jarman, who died in 1994, created a wonderful shingle garden with flotsam, jetsam and hardy beach plants around Prospect Cottage, the wooden shack where he lived. The cottage and garden are still there but are privately owned, so if you decide to visit, please be discreet.

▶ EN; RSPB

■ Woodland

THE UNDERCLIFF, LYME REGIS, DORSET/DEVON BORDER (EN)

A single narrow footpath runs through the Undercliff for five miles along the edge of the cliffs between Lyme Regis and Axmouth. Unstable geology (see **Cliffs**, above) has caused huge landslips, and for 150 years no one has inhabited the Undercliff. Hence its status as a beautiful, natural piece of woodland full of wild flowers and birdsong.

PLACES OF INTEREST

■ Abbotsbury, Dorset

Abbotsbury is a delightful village of thatched houses of mellow stone. It possesses a number of attractions – a great monastic tithe barn nearly 300 feet long, the fourteenth-century St Catherine's Chapel on a hill, the medieval Swannery on the Fleet Lagoon (see **Lagoons**, above), and Abbotsbury Subtropical Gardens just down the lane.

▶ www.abbotsbury.co.uk

■ Dover, Kent

One of the great castles of Britain, Dover Castle was built on its commanding clifftop in 1198 and has been added to ever since – notably underground, where a maze of tunnels dug by Napoleonic prisoners-of-war was used during the Second World War as a command post during the Battle of Dunkirk. Also from Napoleonic

times is the extraordinary Grand Shaft, a triple spiral staircase 140 feet deep.

▶ Dover Castle (EH) ☎ 01304 211067
▶ Grand Shaft ☎ 01304 201066

■ Denge, Dungeness, Kent

Two vast concrete 'ears' and a giant concrete wall rise from the shingle spit of Dungeness. In pre-radar days between the World Wars, these parabolic 'sound mirrors' were the best method of detecting the sounds of enemy aircraft engines in flight, via microphones suspended in the big sound-amplifying bowls.

▶ Denge, Dungeness EH. Visits only on Romney Marsh Countryside Project guided walks.
www.ajg41.clara.co.uk/mirrors/dungeness.html

■ Hurst Castle, near Lymington, Hampshire

One of King Henry VIII's great chain of coast forts that guarded against Spanish and French invasion. Two long wings were added in the 1870s, at a time when French invasion was once more feared.

🚗 At seaward end of 1 mile shingle spit from Milford-on-Sea (EH) ☎ 01590 642344;
www.hurst-castle.co.uk

■ Jurassic Coast, Dorset and East Devon

The 95-mile stretch of coast between Studland Bay in East Dorset and Exmouth in East Devon has been designated a UNESCO World Heritage Site because of its extraordinary geology that runs from the hard pale limestone of the east to the warm red sandstone of the west, with every kind of formation, bend, twist and zigzag in between.

▶ www.jurassiccoast.com

■ Martello Towers, Kent

More coastal fortifications – a chain of 74 squat oval gun towers built along the coasts of Kent and Sussex from 1805 to 1808 to guard against invasion by Napoleon Bonaparte. They were redundant before they were even finished, as the invasion threat had all but vanished by 1808.

▶ www.martello-towers.co.uk
▶ Dymchurch Martello Tower (EH), Dymchurch, Kent
☎ 01304 211067

■ Portsmouth Historic Dockyard, Hampshire

This is England's shrine to a very English hero – Admiral

Horatio Lord Nelson, who inspired the navy he led to maintain British mastery of the seas during the Napoleonic Wars. The centrepiece of the collection is HMS *Victory*, Nelson's flagship, in which he was killed at the moment of victory over the French and Spanish fleets during the Battle of Trafalgar on 21 October 1805.
▶ *023 9286 1533;* **www.flagship.org.uk**

■ D-Day Museum, Southsea, Hampshire

In homage to the Bayeux Tapestry's depiction of the 1066 Norman invasion of Britain, the Overlord Embroidery in Southsea's D-Day Museum shows scenes of the planning, build-up and deceptions and the epic bravery and determination of D-Day on 6 June 1944, the greatest day of invasion in history, when British, American and Canadian troops landed on the beaches of German-occupied Normandy.
▶ *Clarence Esplanade, Southsea 023 9282 7261;* **www.ddaymuseum.co.uk**

RESORTS

■ Bournemouth, Dorset

There are acres of flowerbeds and trees, miles of public gardens and promenades in Bournemouth, an elegant town that developed from a discreet early nineteenth-century retreat for the upper classes into the premier resort of the central south coast. Today Bournemouth is slipping on new apparel as a well-appointed conference venue, but a glance at the crowded sands on hot summer weekends tells you that the town is still the most popular bucket-and-spade resort for miles.
▶ *TIC 01202 451700;* **www.bournemouth.co.uk**

■ Brighton, West Sussex

Under an hour's journey from London, Brighton is the archetypal day-tripper's goodtime seaside resort with a splendid pier, seaside arcades, funfairs and Brighton Rock shops. It's also full of classic Regency architecture from its early nineteenth-century heyday of fashion, notably the Royal Pavilion (*01273 290900;* **www.royalpavilion.org.uk**), a fantastic pleasure dome that the hedonistic George, Prince of Wales, built for himself in 1815.
▶ *TIC 0906 711 2255;* **www.visitbrighton.com**

■ Lyme Regis, Dorset

This small resort on the Dorset/Devon border has distinguished literary connections. The town forms the backdrop to the early scenes of Jane Austen's *Persuasion*; and the Cobb breakwater is the location for the opening scene, memorably caught by Meryl Streep, of the 1981 film *The French Lieutenant's Woman*, based on John Fowles's 1969 novel set in and around Lyme Regis.
▶ *TIC 01297 442138;* **www.lymeregistourism.co.uk**

■ Swanage, Dorset

The little resort of Swanage is a fascinating place to stroll round. George Burt, a local stonemason, grew rich on the Victorian rebuilding of London, and incorporated many wonderful pieces of 'Old London' in the streets and buildings of his home town, including his own overblown but splendid residences of Purbeck House and Durlston Head Castle.
▶ *TIC 01929 422885;* **www.swanage.gov.uk**

■ Weymouth, Dorset

Weymouth became a prosperous resort thanks to its connection with King George III, and is still a West Country favourite. It was through the Dorset port of Melcombe Regis (now part of Weymouth) that the devastating scourge of the Black Death plague entered Britain in 1348 and killed roughly half the population within a year.
▶ *TIC 01305 785747;* **www.weymouth.here-on-the.net**

Useful Websites

www.english-nature.org.uk
www.nationaltrust.org.uk
www.english-heritage.org.uk
www.goodbeachguide.co.uk
www.rspb.org.uk
www.bbc.co.uk/coast

The Exe Estuary to the Severn Estuary

THE WILD WEST

ACTIVITIES

■ Birdwatching

There is fine birdwatching all round the Wild West coast, mostly of summer-nesting seabirds such as kittiwake, guillemot, razorbill, shag and fulmar. The Severn Estuary sees gatherings of up to 5000 shelduck in late summer, mostly in Bridgwater Bay on the Somerset coast, for the annual moult.

■ Fishing

There is wreck, reef and sandbank fishing from Devon harbours such as Salcombe or Dartmouth, day trips after mackerel and whiting, beach fishing in the Severn Estuary with a sturdy rod in hopes of sea bass, or shark trips from Looe and other Cornish ports with an experienced skipper – sea angling of all sorts is a popular West Country sport.

▶ **www.go-fishing.co.uk**

■ Sailing

Small-boat sailing takes place from just about every coastal area with a harbour; notable centres are Salcombe in Devon, Falmouth and Mount's Bay in Cornwall, and Minehead and Watchet on the Somerset shore of the Severn Estuary.

▶ *Cornwall:* **www.porthpeansc.co.uk/sailingclubs**

▶ *Somerset:* **www.sportslinks.info/directory/sailing/somerset.htm**

■ Sea-watching

The warm waters of the south-west are home to a large variety of big fish and marine mammals, among them porbeagles, bottlenosed and whitebeaked dolphins, orcas (killer whales), seals, porpoise and basking sharks.

▶ **www.seawatchfoundation.org.uk**

■ Surfing

Atlantic rollers hit the coasts of North Cornwall and West Devon and funnel into narrow bays, producing the sort of high, reliable waves that surfers love. Tremendous surfing beaches are the neighbouring Newquay and Fistral in Cornwall, Polzeath a little further up the north coast, and Croyde Bay and Woolacombe in Devon on the west of Exmoor.

▶ **www.bbc.co.uk/cornwall/surfing;
www.bbc.co.uk/devon/surfing**

▶ *Surfers Against Sewage:* **www.sas.org.uk**

■ Walking

The South-West Coast Path National Trail runs for 630 miles right round the rim of the south-west peninsula from Poole Harbour in Dorset through South Devon, Cornwall and North Devon to Minehead in Somerset.

▶ **www.swcp.org.uk**

ISLANDS

■ Burgh Island, Devon

On a tiny tidal island off Bigbury-on-Sea an Art Deco classic awaits – the splendid Burgh Island Hotel, where everything from the architectural curves to the bold colours is 1929 and proud of it. Celebrity guests have ranged from Noel Coward (of course!) to Agatha Christie and the Duke of Windsor.

🚗 *At end of B3392, opposite Bigbury-on-Sea, Devon*
📞 *01548 810514;* **www.burghisland.com**

■ Channel Islands

There are light and dark sides to the Channel Islands, slips of British territory off the Normandy coast. Jersey, Guernsey, Alderney and Sark are famous for their festivals of flowers, seafood and walking. The German occupation of the islands during the Second World War has left reminders of those grim days: on Jersey, a German underground hospital built by slave labour, and on Alderney the remains of Lager Sylt, an SS concentration camp for Eastern European slave labourers where hundreds of inmates were beaten, starved, worked and shot.

▶ *German Underground Hospital: Meadowbank, Les Charrieres Malorey, St Lawrence, Jersey* 📞 *01534 863442;* **www.jersey.co.uk/attractions/ughospital**

▶ *Lager Sylt: just east of Alderney airport.*

▶ *Jersey, Guernsey, Alderney:* ✈ *From several UK airports;* 🚢 *From Portsmouth, Poole, Weymouth. Sark:* 🚢 *From the other Channel Islands.*

▶ **www.subbrit.org.uk** *and follow links*

■ Lundy, Devon

Lundy rises from the sea 11 miles off Hartland Point, a grass-topped bar of granite 3 miles long with a scattering of lighthouses and a few buildings. Once it was owned by the Heaven family (and known locally as the 'Kingdom of Heaven'); these days it's a property of the Landmark Trust and welcomes visitors, birdwatchers and marine biology enthusiasts. There is one pub, the Marisco Tavern, but no hotel.

🚢 *By boat from Bideford or Ilfracombe; by helicopter from Hartland Point*

▸ *Lundy Shore Office* ☎ *01271 863636;* **www.lundyisland.co.uk**

■ Scilly Isles, Cornwall

Five inhabited islands make up the Scilly archipelago 28 miles west of Land's End: the capital island, St Mary's, with its flower fields and five miles of road; Tresco, the exotic island planted with one of Britain's finest sub-tropical gardens; and rugged, traffic-free St Martin's, St Agnes and Bryher. Thanks to the Gulf Stream, warm seas, early springs and mild winters make a sort of Atlantis-style paradise of the Scilly Isles.

🚢 *From Penzance to St Mary's, and on by boat to the other islands*

✈ *To St Mary's (planes from several UK airports), or St Mary's and Tresco (helicopter from Penzance)*

▸ *Scilly Isles TIC, St Mary's* ☎ *01720 422536*

▸ *Isles of Scilly Museum, St Mary's* ☎ *01720 422337;* **www.iosmuseum.org**

▸ *Tresco Gardens* ☎ *01720 424105;* **www.tresco.co.uk**

■ Steep Holm, Somerset

There are two neighbouring islands in the narrowing throat of the Severn Estuary: low-lying Flat Holm (see page 141), and Steep Holm with its green humpback. Steep Holm has been used by pirates, hermits and military garrisons down the centuries; today it's a nature reserve administered by the Kenneth Allsop Memorial Trust.

▸ ☎ *01934 632307;* **www.steepholm.org**

NATURAL WORLD

■ Beaches

West Country beaches offer a mixture of qualities – warmth, cleanliness, sand, shelter and safety – that is unique in Britain. Several hold the coveted Blue Flag award for European beaches, signifying that they satisfy stringent criteria in water quality, environmental education and information, environmental management, safety and services. Their physical make-up ranges from the sand dunes of Braunton Burrows and Dawlish

Warren (good for sand plants such as yellow-horned poppy and viper's bugloss) to the shingle bar of Slapton Ley and the pristine sands of Cornwall, and vast sand flats, where rag and lug worms, razor shells and countless invertebrates thrive. (See **Resorts**, below, for the best beaches.)

▸ **www.goodbeachguide.co.uk**

▸ **www.blueflag.org**

■ Cliffs

Cliffs of sandstone along the South Devon coast give way to the magnificent Cornish cliffs in their characteristic dark granite, reverting to sandstone on the coast of North Devon before trending away into the mud flats and limestone promontories of the Somerset shore.

■ Estuaries

Estuaries mark the start, middle and end of the Wild West coast. The estuary of the River Exe is a prime birdwatching spot thanks to wide mud flats exposed each falling tide, especially around the great sandspit of Dawlish Warren (EN), a National Nature Reserve. The coast of north-west Devon is split by the combined estuary of the Two Rivers, Taw and Torridge, where Henry Williamson set many scenes in his 1928 wildlife masterpiece *Tarka The Otter*. As for the Severn Estuary, it is the most extensive, dynamic and dramatically tidal of all British estuaries.

■ Lagoons

Slapton Ley National Nature Reserve, trapped behind the shingle bar of South Devon's Slapton beach, forms the West Country's biggest freshwater lake – a paradise for birds all year round, including the largest UK population of the very rare Cetti's warbler.

🚗 *On A379 between Dartmouth and Torcross*

▸ *Slapton Ley NNR* ☎ *01548 580685;* **www.slnnr.org.uk**

■ Sand dunes

On the northern shore of the Two Rivers estuary (see **Estuaries**, above), Braunton Burrows comprises four miles of sand dunes spattered with wild flowers that include marsh helleborine, yellow-horned poppy, marsh pennywort and round-leaved wintergreen. The Burrows and their surrounding coast are so ecologically important that 7700 acres have been designated Britain's first UNESCO World Biosphere Reserve.

🚗 *Off B3231 at Braunton near Barnstaple*

PLACES OF INTEREST

■ A La Ronde, Exmouth, Devon

When spinster cousins Mary and Jane Parminter took a ten-year-long Grand Tour at the end of the eighteenth century, they came back home inspired by Italian church architecture and set about creating their own octagonal basilica of a house near Exeter. Then they decorated its internal surfaces with feathers, shells and seaweed. A splendidly eccentric folly.

▶ *A La Ronde (NT), Exmouth* ✆ *01395 265514; booking advised*

■ Cape Cornwall

It was on the Seven Stones reef off Cape Cornwall that the tanker *Torrey Canyon* and her cargo of 120,000 tons of crude oil came to grief on 18 March 1967. In spite of efforts by the RAF to bomb the wreck and spray the oil with detergent, it spilt over an area of 270 square miles of sea and came ashore along more than 100 miles of Cornish coastline. Between oil, chemicals and combustibles the pollution killed 25,000 seabirds and countless fish, shellfish and other marine organisms.

■ Dartmouth, Devon

One of the West Country's most attractive towns, Dartmouth has plenty of history packed into its narrow, twisty streets and cobbled byways. It was the port of embarkation for twelfth-century Crusaders, and for great Tudor adventurers and explorers such as Sir Walter Raleigh and Sir Humphrey Gilbert. There's a memorial to the Pilgrim Fathers at picturesque Bayards Cove, where they put in for repairs to *Mayflower* and *Speedwell* on their epic voyage to the New World in 1620.

▶ *TIC* ✆ *01803 834224*

■ Land's End, Cornwall

In spite of its modern makeover as a tourist theme park, Land's End retains its magic. Approaching on an out-of-season day along the coast path that bypasses the tourist attractions, you can dream alone among the pinnacles that slope into the Atlantic as a final full-stop to mainland Britain.

▶ *Tourist information* ✆ *0870 458 0099;*
www.landsend-landmark.co.uk

■ Lizard Peninsula, Cornwall

Lizard Point is the southernmost point of mainland Britain, but there is more to the blunt-tipped Lizard Peninsula than that. Ancient standing stones and satellite dishes stand side-by-side on Goonhilly Downs, the cliffs of Kynance Cove gleam with the rainbow colours of serpentine rock, and up on the Helford River you can find the tree-hung inlet named Frenchman's Creek, inspiration for Daphne Du Maurier's eponymous romantic novel.

■ Lost Gardens of Heligan, Pentewan, Cornwall

The Victorian exotic gardens at Heligan with their pineapple beds, tree ferns and melon houses lay overgrown and forgotten in their sheltered valley until 1990, when they were rediscovered by Tim Smit and John Nelson. A painstaking restoration has seen them recover their full glory.

▶ *Pentewan, St Austell* ✆ *01726 845100;*
www.heligan.com

■ Lynton and Lynmouth, Devon

Lynton perches high in a cleft of the Exmoor coast; Lynmouth lies on the shore below. A Victorian cliff railway powered by water and gravity connects the twin villages. Lynmouth suffered a devastating flood disaster in August 1952, when 34 people drowned in the swollen waters of the West Lyn River. Another famous episode is the rescue adventure of January 1899, when the weather was too bad to launch the Lynmouth lifeboat to assist the endangered cargo ship *Forrest Hall*. Undaunted, the lifeboatmen spent all night dragging the boat on her heavy, wheeled carriage up and across the stormy moors to launch her from Porlock, 13 miles away.

▶ *Lynton and Lynmouth cliff railway* ✆ *01598 753486;*
www.cliffrailwaylynton.co.uk
▶ *TIC* ✆ *01598 752225;*
www.lynton-lynmouth-tourism.co.uk

■ Polperro, Cornwall

The archetypal Cornish fishing village: steep narrow roads, sturdy granite houses, a sheltered little harbour, a maze of tiny, flowery back lanes, and plenty of smuggling and shipwreck stories.

▶ *Polperro Heritage Museum* ✆ *01503 272423*

■ Plymouth, Devon

Plymouth is a great seaport, home base of buccaneering adventurers such as Sir Francis Drake and Captains Frobisher and Hawkins, and point of departure for the Pilgrim Fathers in 1620 and for James Cook on his 1772 South Seas voyage. Drake's statue stands on Plymouth Hoe. The Royal Citadel is a magnificent range of defensive walls and strongpoints, built between 1665 and 1670 to guard the harbour against the Dutch.

▶ *TIC* ✆ *01752 266030*

■ St Michael's Mount, Cornwall

The craggy rock of St Michael's Mount rises dramatically from the sea in Mount's Bay, topped by a great grey castle – one of the West Country's most distinctive sights. The castle, occupying the site of a twelfth-century Benedictine monastery, was converted into a fine country house in the seventeenth century. You can reach the Mount and its bustling little village by causeway at low tide, or by boat from Marazion.

▶ *NT* ✆ *01736 710507; tide times* ✆ *01736 710265*

RESORTS

■ Ilfracombe, Devon

Ilfracombe, situated where the North Devon coast turns east into the Bristol Channel, benefits from beautiful sandy beaches. Fine Victorian houses and hotels huddle round the tight little harbour, which is guarded by the ever-shining light in the fourteenth-century St Nicholas's Chapel on Lantern Hill.

▶ *TIC* ✆ *01271 863001*

■ Newquay, Cornwall

Newquay is North Cornwall's premier resort, a big town which caters for all ages and stages. The wide beach is popular with paddlers, sandcastlers and learner surfers. Overlooking all is the white-painted Huer's House, from which a lookout would shout and wave to let the town's fishermen know that a shoal of pilchards was on the way.

▶ *TIC* ✆ *01637 854020*

■ St Ives, Cornwall

There has been a thriving artists' colony at St Ives for nearly 100 years, and no wonder. The clear north light, the charms of the grey-roofed fishing town and the beautiful surroundings of sand, sea and rock have attracted painters (Alfred Wallis, Ben Nicholson), sculptors (Dame Barbara Hepworth) and potters (Bernard Leach) to West Cornwall.

▶ *TIC* ✆ *01736 796297*

▶ *Tate St Ives* ✆ *01736 796226*

▶ *Barbara Hepworth Museum & Sculpture Garden* ✆ *01736 796226*

■ Torbay, Devon

The conglomerate resort of Torbay is made up of three towns: traditional Paignton with its fine beach and green, the Victorian-flavoured Torquay that will be forever associated with John Cleese and *Fawlty Towers*, and the more salty charms of the fishing town of Brixham.

▶ *TIC* ✆ *0906 680 1268 (calls are charged);* **www.theenglishriviera.co.uk**

Useful Websites

www.english-nature.org.uk
www.nationaltrust.org.uk
www.english-heritage.org.uk
www.wildlifetrusts.org
www.rspb.org.uk
www.countryside.gov.uk
www.goodbeachguide.co.uk
www.bbc.co.uk/coast

The Severn Estuary to Cardigan Bay

TIME AND TIDE

ACTIVITIES

■ Rock climbing

Limestone and volcanic rock make the South Wales cliffs excellent for climbing in several places. St Govan's Head near Bosherston in Pembrokeshire is one of the best areas, but is sometimes closed due to MoD firing practice (☎ *01646 662367*) or bird-nesting restrictions (☎ *01437 775213*). The limestone climbs around St David's Head are excellent, too.

▶ **www.visitpembrokeshire.com**

■ Birdwatching

There are several first-class birdwatching sites. Two notable ones side by side are up along the Severn Estuary at Magor Marsh for breeding snipe, reed bunting, kingfisher and marsh warbler, and the neighbouring Newport Wetlands for bittern, short-eared owl, hen harrier and dozens of duck species in winter. The tip of Worms Head on the Gower Peninsula is excellent for puffin, guillemot, shearwater and other seabirds. Bitterns have been heard and seen among the reeds of the Oxwich National Nature Reserve's pools.

▶ **www.rspb.org.uk/wales/reserves**

■ Sailing and windsurfing

Out in the west of Pembrokeshire winds, waves and large sandy beaches create a wonderful area for sailing, windsurfing and board surfing. There are teaching centres at Dale on Milford Haven inlet and at Broad Haven on St Bride's Bay.

■ Walking

The beautiful and not-too-challenging Pembrokeshire Coast Path National Trail runs for 186 miles from Amroth near Tenby to St Dogmaels near Cardigan. You can walk it in long sections, or use it as a basis for short round walks; but however you do it, it's by far the best way to get to know this coast.

▶ **www.pembrokeshirecoast.org.uk**

ISLANDS

■ Burry Holms, West Glamorgan

Burry Holms is a sandy islet off the north end of Rhossili Beach, accessible at low tide, with traces of a medieval hermit's cell and of an early fortified camp.

■ Caldey, Pembrokeshire

Caldey is the most easterly of the five main Pembrokeshire islands. There's a monastery of the Reformed Cistercian Order, whose monks make perfume and chocolate for sale to visitors; also a lovely wild coastline. With a bit of patience and luck, you may see seals on the ocean swells below.

▶ **www.caldey-island.co.uk**

▶ *Tenby Harbour* ☎ *01834 842296, for boat-crossing information*

■ Flat Holm, South Glamorgan

Along with its twin island of Steep Holm (see page 137), the low-lying island of Flat Holm occupies the throat of the Severn Estuary. On the island is a visitor centre, the ruins of a quarantine hospital, some rusty nineteenth-century cannon, and many thousands of black-backed gulls.

🚢 *From Barry; contact Flat Holm Society* ☎ *01446 747661;* **www.flatholm.co.uk**

■ Grassholm, Pembrokeshire

Grassholm, seven miles west of Skomer, is an RSPB reserve thanks to the 80,000 gannets that nest there, giving the island the aspect of a dome-shaped white wedding cake. Ronald Lockley (see **Skokholm**, below) and his bride Doris honeymooned on Grassholm, with only the gannets for company.

🚢 *From Dale* ☎ *01646 603110*

▶ *RSPB Cymru:* **www.rspb.org.uk/wales**

■ Ramsey, Pembrokeshire

Eight miles north of Skomer rise the two hills of Ramsey Island, an RSPB reserve with a full complement of seabirds and a colony of the very rare chough, a black bird with strikingly scarlet beak and legs. Sea cows give birth on the island's beaches in late summer.

🚢 *By boat from St Justinian's* ☎ *01437 721721 or 721686*

▶ **www.ramseyisland.co.uk**

■ Skokholm, Pembrokeshire

In 1930 writer Ronald Lockley published *Dream Island*, an account of his life and work with the birds on tiny Skokholm. Today small numbers of visitors are allowed onto the mile-long island to revel in the peace and quiet – shattered at night in the breeding season, when Skokholm's 50,000 resident Manx shearwaters return from the sea, screeching and calling, to their island burrows.

🚢 *From Martinshaven; contact Wildlife Trust West Wales* ☎ *01437 765462*

■ Skomer, Pembrokeshire

Skomer lies just across Broad Sound from Skokholm. The island measures less than two miles long, yet plays host to more than 100,000 Manx shearwaters, the world's largest colony of these seabirds. Skomer also has kittiwakes, fulmars, puffins, seals – and 25,000 rabbits.

🚢 *From Martinshaven; contact Wildlife Trust West Wales* ☎ *01437 765462*

■ Sully Island, South Glamorgan

A rocky, uneven causeway leads onto the tidal blob of Sully Island. Defended by the tide and with clear views all round, Sully Island was a stronghold for the Iron Age folk who mounded the earthen ramparts, and for seventeenth-century pirates who would prey on Bristol Channel shipping.

▸ *Access on foot from Swanbridge, off B4267 at Sully near Barry*
▸ *Wildlife Trust West Wales* ☎ *01437 765462*

NATURAL WORLD

■ Beaches

South Wales is rich in wonderful sandy beaches. Good examples of those that hold the coveted Blue Flag award (see page 137, **Natural World, Beaches**) are Southerndown in South Glamorgan; Pembrey in Carmarthenshire; Port Einon on the Gower Peninsula; and Saundersfoot, Tenby, Whitesands Bay and Newgale in Pembrokeshire.

▸ **www.seasideawards.org.uk**

■ Caves

The Gower Peninsula is particularly well supplied with caves, many of which are accessible, but caution is needed, along with an understanding of their historical, archaeological and wildlife importance. The best known is Paviland Cave between Port Einon and Rhossili, where in the 1820s the 'Red Lady of Paviland' was excavated – in fact, the ochre-covered skeleton of an important

Stone Age man, buried with goods of bone and ivory and with seashell necklaces.

▸ *National Trust Warden* ☎ *01792 390636*
(call before attempting to enter caves);
www.explore-gower.co.uk/caves

■ Dunes

Kenfig Burrows form a superb dune system between Porthcawl and Port Talbot. Half buried in the sands are the remains of a tower – all that is left of the Norman castle that once dominated the prosperous town of Kenfig, now smothered beneath the dunes.

🚗 *B4283 near Pyle, north of Porthcawl (M4, Jct 37)*

■ Estuaries

The Severn Estuary is Britain's finest example, a mighty tideway with the second highest tidal range in the world. The Severn Bore phenomenon, a miniature tidal wave that rolls 30 miles inland, is best seen just downriver of Gloucester at Stonebench or Minsterworth, on a high spring tide.

▸ **www.severn-bore.co.uk**

■ Natural harbours

Milford Haven in Pembrokeshire is a huge natural harbour, sheltered from Atlantic storms, with deep water and enough room for a tanker to manoeuvre – hence the development of much of its shoreline as a complex of oil refineries, storage and onward transmission facilities.

■ Promontories

Worms Head sticks far out into the sea from the southern end of Rhossili Beach. The Norsemen named the promontory wurm, a dragon, with good reason – the double hump resembles a swimming sea monster. Seabirds throng the seaward end, which you reach after a rocky causeway scramble. Keep an eye on the tide times – the causeway is only exposed for two hours each side of low tide.

▸ *Rhossili Visitor Centre (NT)* ☎ *01792 390707*

■ Rockpools

The Gower Peninsula is famous for rockpooling, not just for kids with a shrimp net, but for serious students of shore life. The Mumbles, Caswell Bay, Port Einon and Rhossili are among the hotspots where you might expect to find many anemone species, brittle star, sea urchin, crabs, limpets and prawns; plus rockpool fish such as bullhead, goby, weever fish and blenny.

■ Sea stacks

The Stack Rocks rise like a series of steps from the sea just west of St Govan's Head on the south Pembrokeshire coast. The tallest is over 150 feet high. The Welsh call them Elegug or Guillemot Stacks, referring to the seabirds that throng them: razorbills, kittiwakes and fulmars as well as guillemots.

🚗 *Off B4319 east of Castlemartin*

■ Wetlands

The Burry Inlet on the north side of the Gower peninsula has RAMSAR status as a wetland of international importance. Learn all about it in the National Wetlands Centre overlooking the mud flats and sands opposite Llanelli.

▸ *National Wetlands Centre Wales* 📞 *01554 741087*

PLACES OF INTEREST

■ Abercastle, Pembrokeshire

The 4500-year-old cromlech or stone tomb of Carreg Samson stands magnificently on the cliffs above Abercastle Bay. White quartz nuggets gleam in its 15-foot-long capstone, which lies poised on the tips of the three remaining 'legs' or kerbstones of the tomb.

🚗 *Off A487 between St David's and Fishguard*

■ Bosherston, Pembrokeshire

Just below the village of Bosherston lies a series of ponds, on whose surface water lilies bloom from June through the summer. Lord Cawdor created the ponds in the eighteenth century by damming a sea inlet. The waterproof marl lining of the ponds has enriched the water with lime, so many unusual species of aquatic plants grow there.

🚗 *Off B4319 east of Castlemartin*

■ Cardiff

Until the 1980s Cardiff's docklands was a run-down area. Now Cardiff Bay has been spruced up and smartened up with new housing, museums, shops, restaurants and night spots. The barrage (completed in 1999 to create a 500-acre freshwater lake and eight miles of new waterfront for development), which closed off the bay from the sea, turned a previously estuarine

area of mud flats into a freshwater environment, some of which is being managed for wildlife.

▸ *The Tube, Cardiff Bay's Visitor Centre* 📞 *029 2046 3833*
▸ *Cardiff Bay Barrage* 📞 *029 2087 7900*

■ Dunraven, South Glamorgan

A superb sandy beach, fine cliffs, and a big walled garden telling the story of gardening fashions through the ages. The garden is all that's left of Dunraven Castle, a house with a tremendous history – the best story of which concerns local smuggler Mat of the Iron Hand, and the cruel revenge he took on the master of Dunraven, who had once betrayed him to the excise men, an incident in which Mat lost his hand. The smuggler bided his time until he found the Earl's son shipwrecked on Dunraven Beach. There Mat killed the boy and completed his long drawn-out vengeance.

🚗 *Off B4524 east of Ogmore-by-Sea*

■ Glamorgan Heritage Coast

A walk along the Glamorgan Heritage Coast footpath from Llantwit Major to Ogmore-by-Sea is a sheer delight. This coast has been preserved free of roads and ugly development, so that you stroll the cliffs and rocky beaches surrounded by peace, quiet and natural beauty.

▸ *Gower Heritage Centre, Parkmill* 📞 *01792 371206;*
www.goweraonb.org

■ Laugharne, Carmarthenshire

The boathouse in which Dylan Thomas lived and the adjacent garage shed in which he wrote *Under Milk Wood* and other poems are preserved at Laugharne, overlooking the Taf Estuary in a most beautiful spot.

▸ 📞 *01994 427420*

■ Oxwich, Gower, West Glamorgan

Oxwich Beach is a beautiful stretch of pale sand backed by dunes and pools so rich ecologically that they are managed as Oxwich National Nature Reserve. Just up the lane stands Oxwich Castle, a sixteenth-century fortified manor house with a fine dovecot.

▸ *CADW* 📞 *01792 390359*

■ Pendine Sands, Carmarthenshire

On 3 March 1927 John Parry-Thomas was killed at the wheel of his 27-litre Higham Special car 'Babs', trying to break the world land-speed record of 174.883 mph on the eight-mile-long Pendine Sands. Babs was buried in the dunes, and remained entombed until 1969 when she was disinterred and painstakingly restored.

▶ *Pembrey Country Park* ✆ *01554 834443*

■ St David's, Pembrokeshire

St David's, the smallest city in the UK, is dominated by its fine late Norman cathedral, which contains the shrine of St David, national saint of Wales. Nearby stands the ruined but still impressive medieval Bishop's Palace.

▶ *St Davids TIC, National Park Visitor Centre* ✆ *01437 720392*

■ St David's Head, Pembrokeshire

The Pembrokeshire Coast Path National Trail runs all the way round St David's Head and is by far the best way to appreciate this rugged promontory with an Iron Age stronghold at its outer extremity.

■ St Govan's Chapel, Pembrokeshire

There are many medieval chapels in Britain, but none in a more striking location. Seventy-four worn stone steps lead down from St Govan's Head to a tiny slate-roofed chapel, built precariously into a crack in the cliffs. It stands on the site of the cell of St Govan, a sixth-century Irish hermit and itinerant preacher.

🚗 *Just south of Bosherston (see page 143)*

■ Swansea

After decades of decay following bomb damage in the Second World War, Swansea is coming to life again with a revamped dock area that features a new Welsh National Maritime Museum, a National Waterfront Museum focusing on the Industrial Revolution in Wales, and a Dylan Thomas Centre, which probes the rumbustious life of Wales's national poet, a local boy.

▶ *Dylan Thomas Centre* ✆ *01792 463980*
▶ *National Waterfront Museum* ✆ *01792 459640*

RESORTS

■ Barry Island, South Glamorgan

Pleasure park, arcades, funfairs, scenic railway and a sandy beach – Barry Island is a real old-style all-action resort serving Cardiff and the South Wales Valleys.

▶ *TIC* ✆ *01446 747171*

■ Penarth, South Glamorgan

A genteel and low-key Victorian resort with a nice esplanade for strolling and good views out over the Bristol Channel.

▶ *TIC (seasonal)* ✆ *020 2070 8849*

■ Porthcawl, Mid Glamorgan

Porthcawl is a former coal port that reinvented itself in the twentieth century as a seaside resort, thanks to its fine sands. Porthcawl Royal Golf Course attracts golfers from far and wide, and Rest Bay has become a great surfing centre.

▶ *TIC* ✆ *01656 786639*

■ Tenby, Pembrokeshire

Tenby is a pretty little town of narrow streets and friendly local shops, cradled by medieval town walls and set around a small harbour. Tenby boasts four beaches and a range of sand dunes with rare plants, with the Pembrokeshire Coast Path leading away along the cliffs in both directions.

▶ *Tenby TIC* ✆ *01834 842404*

Useful Websites

www.ccw.gov.uk

www.pembrokeshirecoast.org.uk

www.rspb.org.uk/wales

www.wildlifetrusts.org.uk/wtsww

www.cadw.wales.gov.uk

www.bbc.co.uk/coast

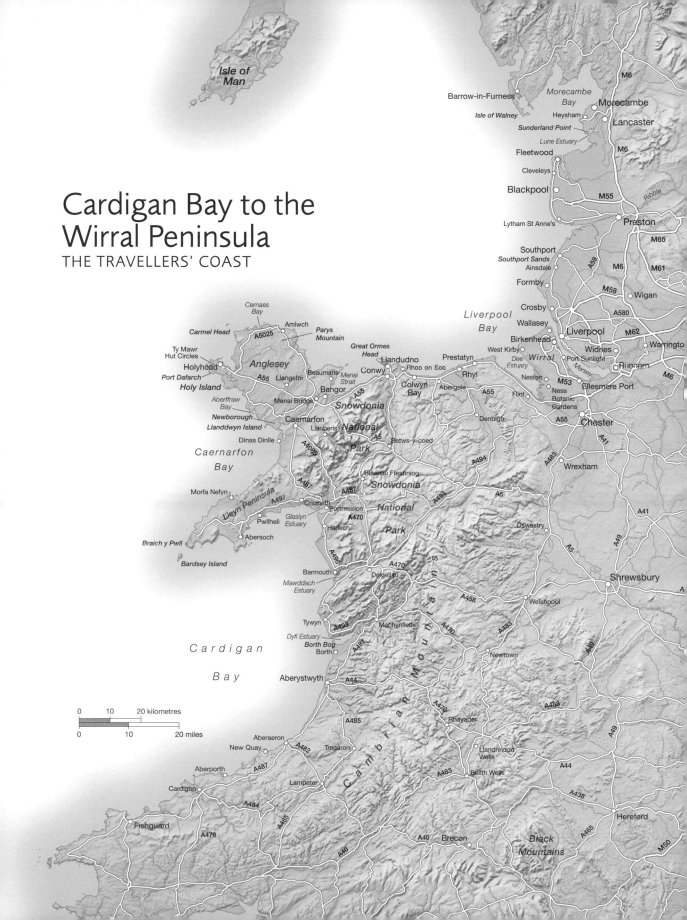

Cardigan Bay to the
Wirral Peninsula
THE TRAVELLERS' COAST

Isle of
Man

Barrow-in-Furness
*Morecambe
Bay*
Morecambe
Isle of Walney
Heysham
Lancaster
Sunderland Point
Lune Estuary
Fleetwood
Cleveleys
Blackpool
M6
M6
M55
M65
Lytham St Anne's
Preston
M6
Southport
M61
Southport Sands
Ainsdale
A59
M6
Formby
M58
Wigan
Crosby
A580
*Liverpool
Bay*
Wallasey
Liverpool
M62
Warringto
*Cemaes
Bay*
Amlwch
Birkenhead
Widnes
Carmel Head
A5025
*Parys
Mountain*
West Kirby
Port Sunlight
Runcorn
M6
*Great Ormes
Head*
Llandudno
Wirral
*Dee
Estuary*
Mersey
*Ty Mawr
Hut Circles*
Holyhead
Anglesey
Conwy
Rhos on Sea
Prestatyn
Neston
M53
Ellesmere Port
Port Dafarch
A55
Llangefni
Beaumaris
Rhyl
Ness
Botanic
Gardens
Holy Island
A55
*Menai
Strait*
Colwyn
Bay
Abergele
Flint
*Aberffraw
Bay*
Bangor
A55
A55
Chester
Menai Bridge
Snowdonia
Denbigh
A55
Newborough
Caernarfon
A41
Llanddwyn Island
Llanberis
National
A5
A494
A483
Dinas Dinlle
A4085
Park
Betws-y-coed
Wrexham
Caernarfon
Bay
A5
Blaenau Ffestiniog
Snowdonia
A494
Oswestry
Morfa Nefyn
A487
A5
A41
National
A470
Criccieth
Portmeirion
A49
Lleyn Peninsula
A497
Park
Pwllheli
*Glaslyn
Estuary*
Harlech
A470
A488
Braich y Pwll
Absersoch
A496
Shrewsbury
Bardsey Island
Welshpool
A458
Barmouth
Dolgellau
*Mawddach
Estuary*
A470
A470
A483
A489
Tywyn
A493
Machynlleth
Dyfi Estuary
A487
Newtown
Borth Bog
Borth
A489
Cardigan
Aberystwyth
A44
A470
Bay
A488
A485
Rhayader
A49
Cambrian Mountains
20 kilometres
Aberaeron
A482
Tregaron
A483
Llandrindod
Wells
New Quay
A44
Aberporth
A487
A483
Builth Wells
20 miles
Lampeter
Cardigan
A484
A438
A485
Fishguard
A478
A40
Brecon
A465
Hereford
*Black
Mountains*
M50

0   10   20 kilometres

0   10   20 miles

ACTIVITIES

■ Birdwatching

With such a rugged coast, facing both west and north, seabird watching is good everywhere; while the estuaries that cut into the coast ensure excellent wader numbers. Two especially rewarding sites are Lavan Sands on the Menai Strait for divers and ducks, including red-breasted merganser and great crested grebe, and the Dee Estuary for waders in their millions and birds of prey such as hen harrier, peregrine and merlin.

▶ **www.deeestuary.co.uk/neshore**

■ Fishing

Almost every little harbour and holiday village along the Travellers' Coast offers sea fishing trips after pollack, mullet, bass and more; also wreck fishing. In the vicinity of Cardigan at the mouth of the River Teifi, you may see fishermen using coracles – traditional round boats light enough to carry.

▶ **www.fishing.visitwales.com**

■ Sea-watching

Atlantic grey seals thrive in Cardigan Bay; a good place to see them close up, in the sea or on the rocks, is at Cardigan Island Farm Park at the mouth of the River Teifi, where the cows have their pups in late summer. Look for bottlenosed dolphins around New Quay in the summer months; they operate in groups or 'pods', and can be seen cavorting and leaping out of the waves.

▶ **www.cardiganisland.com**

▶ **www.seawatchfoundation.org.uk**

■ Surfing

The Isle of Anglesey has many good surfing beaches on its south-west coast; examples are Aberffraw, Rhosneigr and Cable Bay.

▶ **www.bbc.co.uk/wales/northwest/sites/surfing**

■ Walking

The North Wales Path runs for 60 miles from Bangor to Prestatyn, either along the coast or on the mountain slopes behind, giving stunning coastal views. The 90-mile Lleyn Path or Pilgrim Trail skirts the rugged Lleyn Peninsula, while further south Borth and Cardigan are linked by the 63-mile Ceredigion Coast Path.

CASTLES

■ Beaumaris Castle, Anglesey

The last of King Edward I's 'Iron Ring' of fortresses to subdue the rebellious Welsh, Beaumaris was begun on the Menai Strait in 1295. With four miles of defences and 16 bastions, the castle was at the cutting edge of military design. Today it seems the most romantic of places with its pale stone walls.

▶ *CADW* ✆ *01248 810361*

■ Caernarfon Castle, Gwynedd

Caernarfon is the daddy of them all, a mighty fortress begun in 1283 to guard the southern part of the Menai Strait. The huge curtain walls and octagonal towers look impregnably strong, an impression confirmed by the facts: a garrison of just 28 men defied Owain Glyndwr and hundreds of besiegers in 1403 and 1404.

▶ *CADW* ✆ *01286 677617*

■ Conwy Castle, Conwy

Conwy Castle, another of Edward I's 'Iron Ring', was begun in 1283, the same year as Caernarfon. The castle is irregularly shaped to take account of the underlying rock, but it gives the impression of symmetry with its tall drum towers. Conwy town walls, dating from the same era, are a mile in length and offer a memorable stroll with wonderful views.

▶ *CADW* ✆ *01492 592358*

■ Flint Castle, Flintshire

Flint Castle, the founding castle of the 'Iron Ring', is not as complete as the others, but standing over the moody mud flats of the Dee Estuary with its great donjon or keep and its dark shattered walls, it has a uniquely brooding presence.

▶ *CADW* ✆ *01352 733078*

■ Harlech Castle, Gwynedd

When Harlech Castle was begun in 1283, the waters of Tremadog Bay lapped its foundation rock, and the fortress with its great gateway and 40-foot walls was supplied by boat through a sea gate. Today it overlooks sand dunes from its spectacular position on the summit of its crag.

▶ *CADW* ✆ *01766 780552*

ISLANDS

■ Anglesey

The big ragged-shaped island of Anglesey was a centre of the Druidic religion before the Romans crushed it, and deep history buffs can find many standing stones and ancient tombs scattered over the island's rolling landscape. Surfers enjoy the bays of the south-west coast, while lovers of places with long names make straight for Llanfairpwllgwyngyllgogerych wyrndrobwllllantysiliogogogoch ('the church of St Mary in the hollow of the white hazel near a fierce whirlpool and St Tysilio near the red cave').

▸ *TIC (01407 762622;*

www.anglesey-history.co.uk

■ Bardsey, Gwynedd

Out off the tip of the Lleyn Peninsula, Bardsey has been a place of Christian pilgrimage for some 1400 years. Today you can travel by boat to land on Bardsey and admire the thirteenth-century abbey tower, the tall lighthouse, the ancient hut remains and the bird observatory of the Island of 20,000 Saints.

From Porth Meudwy or Pwllheli; contact Bardsey Island Trust (08458 112233; **www.bardsey.org**

■ Hilbre Islands, Merseyside

The three Hilbre Islands lie in the Dee Estuary off West Kirby on the Wirral Peninsula. You can walk out at low tide to the little sandstone ledges, following a set course through the treacherous sands, to visit the bird observatory on Hilbre, the biggest of the three.

▸ **www.deeestuary.co.uk/hilbre**

NATURAL WORLD

■ Beaches

Good sandy beaches abound all along the Travellers' Coast, many of them having earned the Blue Flag award for cleanliness – examples are Aberporth, Borth and Tresaith in Ceredigion (Cardiganshire); Criccieth, Tywyn and Dinas Dinlle near Caernarfon in Gwynedd; and Llandwyn at Newborough, Porth Dafarch at Trearddur Bay and Traeth Mawr at Cemaes Bay in Anglesey.

■ Bogs

Many plant species thrive in the peaty soil of Borth Bog (Cors Fochno) in the Dyfi Estuary. The UK's biggest estuarine raised bog nourishes various rushes and ferns, bog myrtle, bog rosemary, heather, cotton grass, orchids and insectivorous plants such as sundews.

■ Coast

The coast of Cardigan Bay is of exceptional landscape and conservation value, and four sections in particular are protected under the Ceredigion Heritage Coast designation: Borth to Clarach, Monk's Cave to Llanrhystud, New Quay to Tresaith and Pen-peles to Gwbert.

■ Estuaries

Of several estuaries that cut into the Travellers' Coast, three are especially impressive. The estuary of the Afon Dyfi, reaching Cardigan Bay at Aberdyfi, is a UNESCO Biosphere Reserve thanks to its grazed saltmarshes and RAMSAR-status wetlands that attract wintering birds in big numbers, the Ynyslas sand dune system, Borth Bog (see **Bogs**, above) and a submarine forest. Birdwatching is excellent along the Mawddach Estuary, a beautiful wooded waterway debouching at Barmouth; and the vast sands and muds of the Dee Estuary are wonderful for geese, ducks, waders and other seabirds.

PLACES OF INTEREST

■ Birkenhead, Wirral

The Historic Warships Trust collection in the East Float at Birkenhead Docks includes two vessels that took part in the 1982 Falklands conflict, the frigate HMS *Plymouth* and the submarine HMS *Onyx*. Also here is Second World War landing craft LCT 7074, a D-Day veteran, and a German U-boat salvaged from the sea floor.

▸ *The Warship Preservation Trust (0151 650 1573;* **www.historicwarships.org**

■ Cantref-y-Gwaelod, Ceredigion

Between Aberystwyth and Borth, the long pebble ridge of Sarn Cynfelyn runs into the sea. Legend says it was once a causeway to Cantref-y-Gwaelod, the 'Lowland Hundred', a fabulous walled city in the sea. Alas, the drunken city governor neglected to shut the sluice-gates, whereupon the sea broke in and engulfed the place. A submarine forest in the area shows that the land did once extend far into the sea – doubtless the source of the legend.

■ Fishguard, Pembrokeshire

Fishguard has had a racy history (see page 38), but these days it is very much a working port with a thriving Irish ferry business to Rosslare in County Wexford.

▶ *TIC* ☎ *01348 872037*

■ Great Orme, Conwy

The round-nosed promontory of the Great Orme sticks out from the North Wales coast at Llandudno. Bronze Age miners dug for copper in a labyrinth of galleries, which you can visit. There's also great seabird-watching on the cliffs.

▶ *Great Orme Mines, Llandudno* ☎ *01492 870447*

■ Holyhead, Anglesey

Situated at the outer edge of the Isle of Anglesey, Holyhead was 'made' when the Chester and Holyhead Railway opened in 1848, bringing the Irish Mail and tens of thousands of passengers to the Irish ferries. Nowadays Holyhead is the chief UK ferryport for Dublin and Dun Laoghaire.

▶ *TIC* ☎ *01407 762622*

■ Lleyn Peninsula, Gwynedd

It's a long walk (90 miles), sometimes difficult but always beautiful, along the Pilgrim Trail that follows the coastline of the Lleyn Peninsula at the north-west shoulder of Wales. This is the best way to appreciate the lonely charms of the rugged, weatherbeaten cliffs and coves of Lleyn, still very much a land apart.

▶ **www.lleyn-wales.co.uk**

■ Menai Strait, Anglesey

Crossing the Menai Strait between mainland Wales and the Isle of Anglesey was always a hazardous undertaking because of swift and dangerous tides, and shifting sands. When Holyhead–Dublin ferry services expanded early in the nineteenth century, it became necessary to improve the difficult and restricted Menai Strait crossing to cope with the huge increase in traffic between mainland and island. Thomas Telford built a suspension bridge in 1826 to carry the improved road high above the treacherous channel, and when the railway arrived it was brought

across the Strait by way of Robert Stephenson's tubular Britannia Bridge (a revolutionary design) in 1850.

■ Ness Botanic Gardens, Wirral

At Neston on the Wirral Peninsula is one of Britain's most interesting botanic gardens. Founded and planted with hundreds of exotic species by Liverpool cotton merchant Arthur Kilpin Bulley, its displays include gentians, rhododendrons, azaleas, camellias and several heathers.

▶ ☎ *0151 353 0123*; **www.nessgardens.org**

■ North Hoyle, Merseyside

Thirty enormous turbines stand in the sea off the Wirral Peninsula, each mast over 200 feet tall. The whirling arms of the North Hoyle wind farm can generate up to 60 megawatts, enough to light 50,000 homes.

■ Parys Mountain, Anglesey

The copper mines on Parys Mountain in Anglesey were in production for at least 3500 years. A trail takes you through the eras from primitive Bronze Age bell pits to the eighteenth-century height of production, when 1500 miners worked here extracting the metal that went to sheath the hulls of the Royal Navy's wooden sailing ships.

▶ *Amlwch Industrial Heritage Trust, visitor centre at Amlwch Port* ☎ *01248 361333*;

www.parysmountain.co.uk

■ Port Sunlight, Wirral

Victorian soap mogul William Lever built this model settlement on the Mersey shore of the Wirral Peninsula for the workers at his Sunlight soap factory. 'Old English', classical, Gothic, Baroque, and Arts and Crafts styles were all employed, and the inhabitants enjoyed light, air and space hitherto unknown to the nineteenth-century urban working class.

▶ **www.portsunlight.org.uk**

■ Portmeirion, Gwynedd

Portmeirion is a fantasy turned into reality: a village composed of examples of architecture selected from sites all over the world. They include a lighthouse, a castle, an Italian campanile and a classical colonnade. It was all the brainchild of architect Sir Clough Williams-Ellis (1883–1978). The famous Portmeirion pottery with its floral and butterfly motifs is sold here. Portmeirion was the setting for the cult 1960s TV series *The Prisoner*. There is a *Prisoner* shop, too.

▶ *℄ 01766 770000;* **www.portmeirion-village.com**

■ **Ty Mawr Mountain Hut Circles, Holyhead, Anglesey**

Situated on the south-west slopes of Holyhead Mountain at the seaward end of Holy Island lies the Ty Mawr hut group. The circular remains of ten Iron Age dwellings and associated metal-working shops lie on a grassy ridge in a most beautiful location.

▶ *CADW-managed*

RESORTS

■ **Aberystwyth, Ceredigion**

Aberystwyth still retains its air of good times beside the sea, as befits a long-established resort. The town is also the 'capital' of Welsh-speaking Wales; both the University of Wales and the National Library of Wales are sited here, and you won't have to go far to hear Welsh being spoken.

▶ *TIC ℄ 01970 612125;* **www.aberystwyth.org.uk**

■ **Barmouth, Ceredigion**

Still the choice of holidaymakers from the Midlands of England, Barmouth stands piled on its hillside over a superb stretch of sandy beach. The town overlooks the Mawddach Estuary and the great railway viaduct that strides across on 114 legs of timber.

▶ *TIC ℄ 01341 280787;* **www.barmouth.org.uk**

■ **Llandudno, Conwy**

A real old Victorian resort in a fabulous position under the headland of the Great Orme, Llandudno has vast stretches of sand, a pier nearly half a mile long, and a promenade that offers great views from its crescent sweep along the front.

▶ *TIC ℄ 01492 876413*

■ **New Quay, Ceredigion**

The town of New Quay rises along its green hillsides by way of streets that were once ropewalks. The church holds memorials to mariners of times past, and there's a strong 'marine activity' flavour to the town with its Marine Wildlife Centre, boat trips to see the dolphins, fishing trips, sailing from the harbour

and several nearby sandy beaches.

▶ *TIC ℄ 01545 560865;* **www.new-quay.com**

■ **Rhyl and Prestatyn, Denbighshire**

Twin 'Big Fun' resorts just west of the Dee Estuary with huge sandy beaches, funfairs, watersports, golf and bowls, and a Children's Village full of rides and activities.

▶ *TIC ℄ 01745 355068*

Useful Websites

www.ccw.gov.uk
www.nationaltrust.org.uk
www.cadw.wales.gov.uk
www.goodbeachguide.co.uk
www.wildlifetrusts.org
www.rspb.org.uk/wales
www.countryside.gov.uk
www.castlexplorer.co.uk/list-wales.php
www.castleuk.net/castle_lists_wales
www.bbc.co.uk/coast

Cardigan Bay to the Wirral Peninsula

THE TRAVELLERS' COAST

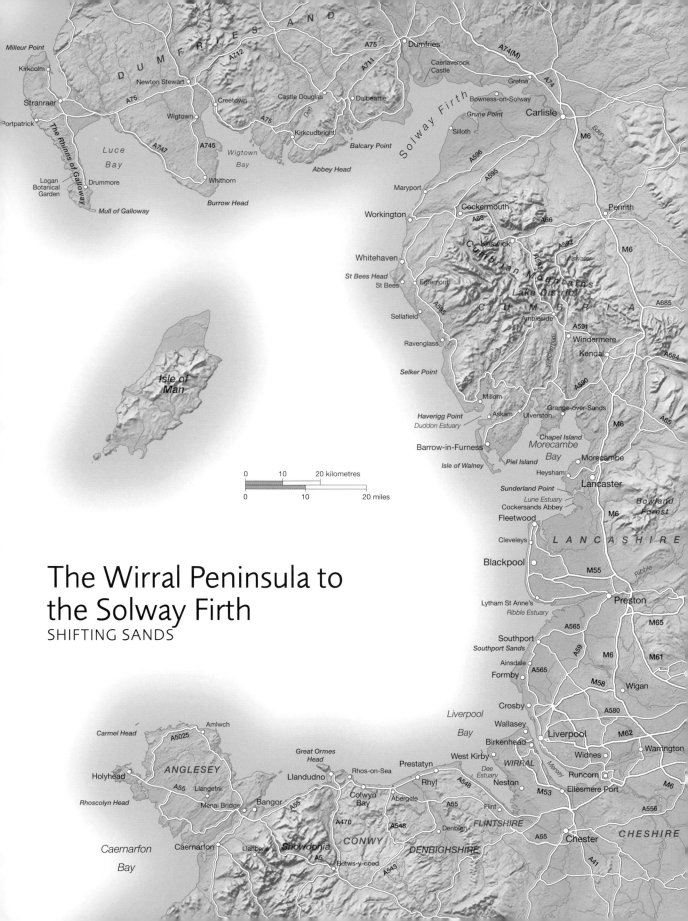

The Wirral Peninsula to the Solway Firth
SHIFTING SANDS

DUMFRIES AND

Milleur Point
Kirkcolm
Stranraer
Portpatrick
The Rhinns of Galloway
Logan Botanical Garden
Drummore
Mull of Galloway

Newton Stewart
A712
A75
Creetown
Castle Douglas
Wigtown
A745
A75
Dee
Kirkcudbright
A747
A75
Luce Bay
Wigtown Bay
Whithorn
Burrow Head
Abbey Head
Balcary Point

Dumfries
A711
Dalbeattie
Caerlaverock Castle
Gretna
Bowness-on-Solway
Grune Point
Silloth
Solway Firth

A74(M)
A74
Carlisle
M6
Eden

Maryport
Cockermouth
A596
A595
A66
A66
Penrith
M6

Workington
Keswick
Cumbrian Mountains
Lake District
Ullswater
A592
A66

Whitehaven
St Bees Head
St Bees
Egremont
Sellafield
A595
CUMBRIA
Ambleside
A685
A591
Windermere
Kendal
A684

Ravenglass
Selker Point
Windermere
A590
A65

Millom
Askam
Ulverston
Grange-over-Sands
M6

Haverigg Point
Duddon Estuary
Barrow-in-Furness
Chapel Island
Morecambe Bay
Morecambe
Piel Island
Heysham
Isle of Walney
Sunderland Point
Lune Estuary
Cockersands Abbey
Lancaster
Bowland Forest
M6

Fleetwood
Cleveleys
LANCASHIRE

Blackpool
M55
Ribble

Lytham St Anne's
Ribble Estuary
Preston
M65

A565
A59
M6
M61

Southport
Southport Sands
Ainsdale
Formby
A565
M58
Wigan

Crosby
A580

Liverpool Bay
Wallasey
Birkenhead
Liverpool
M62
Widnes
Warrington

West Kirby
WIRRAL
Mersey
Runcorn
M53
Ellesmere Port
M6

Carmel Head
Amlwch
A5025
ANGLESEY
Great Ormes Head
Rhos-on-Sea
Prestatyn
Dee Estuary
Neston
A556
CHESHIRE

Holyhead
A55
Llangefni
Llandudno
Rhyl
A548
Flint
Chester
A41

Rhoscolyn Head
Menai Bridge
Bangor
A55
Colwyn Bay
Abergele
A55
FLINTSHIRE
Denbigh
DENBIGHSHIRE

Caernarfon Bay
Caernarfon
Llanberis
Snowdonia
A5
A470
A548
Betws-y-coed
A543
CONWY

Isle of Man

0   10   20 kilometres
0   10   20 miles

ACTIVITIES

■ Birdwatching

The shifting sandbanks and enormous mud flats of the Ribble Estuary, the Solway Firth, Morecambe Bay and the Great Sands of south Lakeland shelter marine worms, shellfish and other invertebrates without number – hence their popularity with coast birds such as oystercatcher, plover, redshank, curlew, knot, dunlin, godwit, tern and black-backed gull. Birdwatching is also first class on the cliffs around St Bees Head in west Cumbria (see **Cliffs**, below).

■ Racing

Each year, generally in early April, Merseyside's Aintree racecourse hosts the world's most famous horse race, the Grand National. Red Rum, the most successful Grand National horse of all time with three wins (1973, 1974 and 1977), used to train by galloping on Southport sands, where you may still see racehorses cantering through the surf.

■ Riding on beaches

If you fancy emulating Red Rum's exploits, you can ride on Formby beach, and also on Ainsdale Beach a little further north.

■ Walking

The nearer you get to the Lake District, the better the coastal walking. The Cumbria Coastal Way runs for 150 miles from Silverdale on Morecambe Bay right up the west Cumbrian coast to Gretna Green on the Scottish border; while from St Bees, halfway up the west Cumbrian coast, the Coast-to-Coast long distance path sets off for Robin Hood's Bay 190 miles away.

▶ *Cumbria Coastal Way:* **www.ramblers.org.uk**
▶ *Coast-to-Coast Walk:* **www.coast2coast.co.uk**

ISLANDS

■ Chapel Island, Cumbria

Chapel Island lies in the sands off the village of Bardsea near Ulverston. You can walk out and back again between tides, but it is essential to take advice on local routes and tides.

■ Isle of Man

The self-governing Isle of Man lies in the Irish Sea some 70 miles from its mainland ferryports of Liverpool and Heysham, a green mountain-backed island measuring 33 miles by 12 miles. There is a lively resort in Douglas; also some pretty villages tucked away, wooded glens leading to the sea, and beautiful walking along the Millennium Way footpath.

🚢 *From Heysham, Liverpool, Belfast, Dublin*
✈ *From many UK regional airports*
▶ *TIC* ☎ *01624 686766*
▶ **www.isle-of-man.com**

■ Piel Island, Cumbria

Piel Island, with its fourteenth-century castle, rises from the sands in the southern crook of the Isle of Walney. One of the treats of a day here is having a drink with the King of Piel; that's the honorary title bestowed on the landlord of the Ship Inn, Piel Island's solitary pub.

▶ *Access: walking over the sands*
🚢 *From Roa Island*
▶ *Piel Castle (EH)*

■ Walney Island, Cumbria

Eleven-mile-long Walney Island, connected to the mainland at Barrow-in-Furness by a bridge, is a long, thin bar of sandstone and pebbles with a hook at each end. Migrating birds often arrive exhausted among the marshes, foreshores and reedy pools of North Walney National Nature Reserve, a great favourite with bird-watchers. South Walney Reserve is well known for its huge gull colonies.

🚌 *A5087 from Barrow-in-Furness*
▶ *EN and Cumbria Wildlife Trust*
▶ **www.walney-island.com**

NATURAL WORLD

■ Beaches

The Sefton Coast is the name for a grand series of beaches that runs for 20 miles from Crosby on the northern outskirts of Liverpool to the Ribble Estuary by way of Formby, Ainsdale and Southport.

▶ **www.seftoncoast.org.uk**

■ Cliffs

The only cliffs of this coast are the red sandstone 'sea ramparts' of west Cumbria. They rise more than 300 feet around St Bees Head, where superb birdwatching includes gannet and shearwater,

guillemot and puffin, fulmar and kittiwake, raven
and peregrine, and England's only breeding colony
of black guillemot, a bird of the Arctic Circle.

▸ *St Bees Head Reserve RSPB* ☎ *01697 351330*

■ Dunes

There are some splendid dune systems along
the coast, supporting natterjack toads, great
crested newts and many rare dune plants. A pick
of the best would include the Ainsdale Sand Dunes
NNR, Cabin Hill NNR, Ainsdale and Birkdale
Sandhills LNR and Ravenmeols Sandhills LNR – all
these on Merseyside – and in Cumbria, the Eskmeals
Nature Reserve at Ravenglass and the Sandscale
Haws NNR (NT) at the southern mouth of the
Duddon Estuary.

■ Estuaries

The enormous sandy saucer of Morecambe Bay
(see **Places of Interest**, below) is the showpiece,
but several other notable estuaries cut into this coast,
including Lancashire's Ribble Estuary with its big mud
and sand flats, the Duddon Estuary of south Cumbria
(see **Places of Interest**, below), and the vast open
miles of the Solway Firth on the border of England
and Scotland where fishermen still go haaf netting,
an ancient practice involving a net mounted on a
frame 18 feet long.

■ Shingle

Grune Point, near Silloth in Cumbria, is a fine, raised
beach of shingle on the south shore of the Solway
Firth, where you can find the spectacular sea holly
with its spiky blue-green leaves and showy flowers
like baby-blue powder puffs.

PLACES OF INTEREST

■ Barrow-in-Furness, Cumbria

Barrow lies out on a limb at the tip of the Furness
Peninsula. The wide streets and handsome architecture show its origin as a Victorian planned town, built
on the back of prosperity from Barrow's great iron and
steel works. These days Barrow houses Britain's most
important shipyard, building nuclear submarines for
the Royal Navy.

▸ *TIC* ☎ *01229 870156*

■ Bowness-on-Solway, Cumbria

There's nothing to see of Hadrian's Wall here today,
but this tiny fishing village was where the mighty
wall that signified the boundary of the Roman
Empire ended in the waters of the Solway Firth.
Today it marks the end of the Hadrian's Wall
Path National Trail.

▸ **www.nationaltrail.co.uk/hadrianswall**

■ Cockersands Abbey, Lancashire

Sandstone archways, sandstone walls and the
outlines of windows eroded by salt winds and
spray are all that's left of the thirteenth-century
Chapter House of Cockersands Abbey. The ruins
stand in a beautiful lonely spot on the south
shore of the Lune Estuary. Only the Gothic whim
of the Daltons of nearby Thurnham Hall saved the
Chapter House from demolition for building stone,
the fate of the rest of Cockersands Abbey – they
had it turned into a family mausoleum during
the eighteenth century.

■ Duddon Estuary, Cumbria

Two unlikely bedfellows, poetry and ironworking,
mark the history of the Duddon Estuary. William
Wordsworth (1770–1850) wrote 34 sonnets to the
River Duddon in the early nineteenth century, when
the estuary was still a peaceful pre-industrial place:
'Majestic Duddon over smooth flat sands/
Gliding in silence with unfettered sweep! . . . '
By the time the great Millom-born poet Norman
Nicholson (1914–87) was writing of seeing
'the slagbanks slant/Like screes sheer into the sand',
his native estuary was fouled by nearly two centuries
of ironworking. These days the ironworks are gone
(though the slagbanks remain) and the Duddon
glides in silence again.

▸ **www.duddon-estuary.org.uk**

■ Liverpool, Merseyside

The dock area of the city has undergone a
transformation since the run-down days of the 1970s.
Now the grand buildings of the Pier Head have a
worthy neighbour in the revitalized Albert Dock area
with its bars, restaurants, shops, tour boats and clutch
of first-class museums including the Merseyside

Maritime Museum, Tate Liverpool, The Beatles Story and the Museum of Liverpool Life.

▶ *TIC* ☎ *0151 237 3925;* **www.visitliverpool.com**

▶ **www.albertdock.com**

▶ **www.liverpoolmuseums.org.uk**

■ Maryport, Cumbria

The fishing town of Maryport on its lonely curve of the Cumbrian coast was the site of a Roman fort and settlement, and the town's Senhouse Museum contains a fine display of Roman inscriptions and sculptures.

▶ *Senhouse Museum* ☎ *01900 816168;*
www.senhousemuseum.co.uk

■ Millom, Cumbria

A former ironworking town on the Duddon Estuary (Millom Folk Museum tells the story), Millom was the home town of the celebrated poet Norman Nicholson (see **Duddon Estuary**, above). There's a blue plaque on the wall of 14 St George's Terrace, the house in which he was born, lived all his life and died.

▶ *TIC* ☎ *01229 716115*

■ Morecambe Bay, Lancashire/Cumbria

These 117 square miles of sand are harvested for their innumerable buried shellfish by humans and birds alike. Walking the sands is a very popular pastime, but extremely dangerous unless you have expert knowledge of local tides, weather, time and route. The best plan is to join one of the walks across the bay led by the official Sands Guide, Cedric Robinson.

▶ *Sands walks details: Morecambe TIC* ☎ *01524 582808 or Grange-over-Sands TIC* ☎ *01539 534026*

▶ **www.morecambebay.com**

■ Ravenglass, Cumbria

Ravenglass faces the Irish Sea across a great wilderness of sands built up by the confluence of three rivers, the Esk, the Mite and the Irt. There's a Roman bathhouse here, and also the seaward terminus of the miniature 15-inch gauge Ravenglass and Eskdale Railway ('The Ratty'), on whose diminutive trains you can chuff up beautiful Eskdale into the mountains.

▶ *Ravenglass and Eskdale Railway* ☎ *01229 717171;*
www.ravenglass-railway.co.uk

■ St Bees, Cumbria

What remains of St Bees Priory, founded in 1120, is a wonderful red sandstone church with an elaborate west door and a cool interior faded to a delicate rose pink. In the south aisle of the church several beautiful old carved stones are displayed. A sandstone cross in the churchyard wall has an effigy of St Michael battling a dragon, a carving that looks more Viking than Norman.

▶ **www.stbees.org.uk**

■ Sellafield, Cumbria

It's the huge scale of everything at Sellafield Nuclear Reprocessing Plant on the Cumbrian coast that's so impressive, plus the setting of timeless mountains and sea, which makes the site such a potent symbol of twentieth-century technology and angst.

▶ *Sellafield Visitors Centre, Seascale* ☎ *01946 727027;*
www.sellafield.com

■ Sunderland Point, Lancashire

Today, only a short street of houses and a handful of old stone warehouses survives at Sunderland Point. But in the eighteenth century, this isolated spot at the mouth of the Lune Estuary, cut off twice every 24 hours by the tide, was the most important port on this coast. Rum, sugar, cotton and other commodities from Britain's New World colonies entered the country here – as did slaves like the young man named Sambo who died on this alien shore. His grave, still decorated with flowers from time to time, lies by a stone field wall on the west side of the Point.

■ Whitehaven, Cumbria

In the 1960s Whitehaven was notoriously run-down and shabby. Then the historic old port and coalmining centre on the Cumbrian coast, a planned Georgian town, began to smarten itself up with money invested by its chief employer, British Nuclear Fuels, based at Sellafield just down the road. These days the fine old buildings have been restored and the town is a fascinating place to stroll through.

▶ *TIC* ☎ *01946 852939*

RESORTS

■ Blackpool, Lancashire

Blackpool is to become a casino town – but when was it ever anything else but a fine, flashy place to spend your money? The era when the cotton towns of Lancashire would shut for the workers' holidays and everyone would go to Blackpool are gone, but the Golden Mile still exerts its seedy charm; the Mighty Wurlitzer and the 3-Deck Wersi organ play for the Tower Ballroom dancers; traditional wooden rollercoasters operate alongside state-of-the-art whiteknuckle screamoramas at the Pleasure Beach funfair – and best of all, the town's Central and South beaches have received the Seaside Flag award (as opposed to the Blue Flag, which goes only to resort beaches) for cleanliness and decent facilities, after decades of dirt and neglect.

▶ *TIC ✆ 01253 292029;* **www.blackpooltourism.com**

▶ *Blackpool Tower:* **www.theblackpooltower.co.uk**

■ Grange-over-Sands, Cumbria

Grange-over-Sands on Morecambe Bay's Kent estuary is the antithesis of Blackpool – a quiet, discreet resort heavy on flower gardens, brass band concerts, birdwatching trips and genteel Edwardian charm.

▶ *TIC ✆ 015395 34026*

■ Southport, Merseyside

Southport is a good old-fashioned beach resort (with a touch more class than Blackpool) that is reinventing itself as a conference venue and golfing centre. However, there's still a great beach for traditional pursuits, a 3650-foot pier (opened in 1860, it's one of the world's oldest iron piers), and Pleasureland theme park with rides scary enough to bring out the teenage screamer in everyone.

▶ *TIC ✆ 01704 533333*

Useful Websites

www.english-nature.org.uk

www.nationaltrust.org.uk

www.english-heritage.org.uk

www.goodbeachguide.co.uk

www.wildlifetrusts.org

www.rspb.org.uk

www.countryside.gov.uk

www.bbc.co.uk/coast

Northern Ireland:
Carlingford Lough to Lough Foyle
BETWEEN A ROCK AND A HARD PLACE

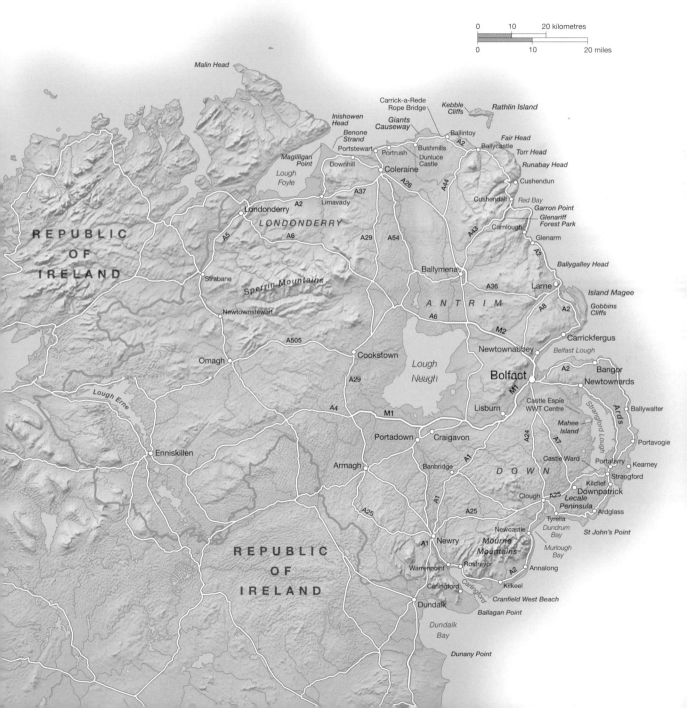

0   10   20 kilometres
0   10   20 miles

Malin Head

Inishowen Head

Carrick-a-Rede Rope Bridge

Kebble Cliffs

Rathlin Island

Giants Causeway

Benone Strand

Ballintoy

Fair Head

Magilligan Point

Portstewart

Bushmills

A2

Ballycastle

Torr Head

Downhill

Portrush

Dunluce Castle

Runabay Head

Lough Foyle

Coleraine

Cushendun

Limavady

A26

A44

Red Bay

Cushendall

Garron Point

Londonderry

A2

A37

A43

Glenariff Forest Park

LONDONDERRY

Carnlough

A5

A6

A29

A54

Glenarm

A2

Ballygalley Head

Strabane

Sperrin Mountains

Ballymena

Newtownstewart

A N T R I M

A36

Larne

Island Magee

A6

Gobbins Cliffs

A505

M2

A8

A2

Omagh

Carrickfergus

Cookstown

Newtownabbey

Belfast Lough

A2

Bangor

Lough Neagh

Belfast

Newtownards

Ballywalter

A29

Castle Espie WWT Centre

REPUBLIC
OF
IRELAND

Lisburn

M1

A24

Mahee Island

Strangford Lough

Ards

Portavogie

Lough Erne

A4

M1

A7

Castle Ward

Portaferry

Kearney

Enniskillen

Portadown

Craigavon

Strangford

D O W N

Kilclief

Armagh

Banbridge

Downpatrick

A1

Clough

A25

Lecale Peninsula

Ardglass

A25

Newcastle

A25

St John's Point

Tyrella

A1

Newry

Dundrum Bay

REPUBLIC
OF
IRELAND

Mourne Mountains

Murlough Bay

Warrenpoint

Rostrevor

A2

Annalong

Carlingford

Carlingford

Kilkeel

Dundalk

Cranfield West Beach

Ballagan Point

Dundalk Bay

Dunany Point

ACTIVITIES

■ Birdwatching

Seabirds, waders and overwintering geese and ducks abound on Northern Ireland's lough-indented coast. Prime wintering sites are Murlough National Nature Reserve at Dundrum Bay in Co. Down for divers, grebe, light-bellied brent geese and greenshank, and Strangford Lough for wigeon, light-bellied brent geese, whooper swans and waders; while in the summer Kebble Cliffs on Rathlin Island hold up to 250,000 breeding seabirds including puffin, razorbill, kittiwake, guillemot and fulmar.

▸ *Dundrum Bay, Co. Down NTNI* ✆ *028 4375 1467*
▸ *Strangford Lough, Co. Down WWT (Wildfowl & Wetlands Centre at Castle Espie)* ✆ *028 9187 4146*
▸ *Rathlin Island Cliffs, Co. Antrim RSPB* ✆ *028 2076 3948*

■ Fishing

Sea fishing is remarkably good because the hot spots have not been overexploited. There are dozens of beaches and promontories for shore anglers. Boat enthusiasts should try Carlingford Lough for tope, Ardglass on the Lecale Peninsula in Co. Down for mackerel, codling, gurnard and whiting, or Portrush in Co. Antrim for ray and turbot. Wreck fishing offers hopes of wrasse, dogfish and big conger.

■ Walking

As with fishing, there has been no over-exploitation. Co. Down's famed Mountains of Mourne are networked with footpaths offering sea views, while the Causeway Coast Path in Co. Antrim lets you wander the spectacular cliffs and shores for 33 miles from Ballycastle to Portstewart via Carrick-a Rede rope bridge, the Giant's Causeway and Dunluce Castle.

▸ *Causeway Coast Path:* **www.waymarkedways.com**

ISLANDS

■ Rathlin Island, Co. Antrim

This L-shaped island lies off Ballycastle. At the western end, Kebble Cliffs are alive with seabirds in summer (see **Activities, Birdwatching**, above). The little village at the landing jetty contains a friendly pub and the small Boat House Museum, which has excellent displays on Rathlin Island's history.

🚢 *Calmac Ferries* ✆ *028 2076 9299*
▸ *Kebble Cliffs birdwatching viewpoint: RSPB warden* ✆ *028 2076 3948*
▸ *Boat House Museum* ✆ *028 2076 3951/2024 (summer only)*

NATURAL WORLD

■ Beaches

There are some beautiful beaches in Northern Ireland, generally with plenty of elbow-room. Beaches that have been awarded Blue Flag status for cleanliness and good facilities are at Cranfield West near Kilkeel and Tyrella near Newcastle in Co. Down; Ballycastle and the three Portrush beaches of East Strand, West Strand and White Rocks in Co. Antrim; and Portstewart Strand and Benone Strand in Co. Derry.

■ Cliffs

The great cliffs of the Antrim coast are famous for their impressive height – up to 800 feet in places – and for the variety of colour imparted by their succession of rock types. The best way to see them is via the A2 Coast Road and its Torr Head scenic diversion.

■ Dunes

The Northern Ireland coast possesses two dune systems of international importance – the 6000-year-old dunes at Murlough Bay, Co. Down, with their rare plants, butterflies and visiting seal population, and those around Magilligan Point at the mouth of Lough Foyle in Co. Derry, bright with sky-blue harebells and fragrant with wild thyme and the vanilla scent of pyramidal orchids.

▸ *Murlough National Nature Reserve NTNI* ✆ *028 4375 1467*
▸ *Magilligan Point Nature Reserve EHSNI* ✆ *028 7776 3982*

■ Glens

The nine Glens of Antrim run roughly parallel in a north-easterly direction, cutting deeply through the basalt to the sea coast. They form a delightful series of diversions from the coast road. Glenariff is the biggest and most popular, and Glenariff Forest Park

offers a number of spectacular ravine paths on
suspended walkways.

▶ *Gleniariff Forest Park* ✆ *028 2955 6000;*
www.forestserviceni.gov.uk/our_forests/glenariff/
glenariff.htm

■ Mountains

Northern Ireland has only one range of coastal
mountains, and they are beauties. The Mountains of
Mourne stand above the coast of Co. Down in a tight
huddle of peaks, very tempting to the walker. Good
leaflet or book guides to Mourne walks are scarce;
Newcastle TIC can offer some material and the
1:25,000 'Mourne Country Outdoor Pursuits' map.

▶ *Newcastle, Co. Down TIC* ✆ *028 4372 2222*
www.walksinthemournes.com

PLACES OF INTEREST

■ Ards Peninsula, Co. Down

Ards Peninsula hangs down like a slightly bent arm
from the shoulder of Co. Down to the east of Belfast,
cradling Strangford Lough (see below) in its armpit.
Its 25-mile east-facing coast is studded with small
fishing villages and unfrequented, windy beaches;
its inner coast looks out onto the great sea lough
and its birds.

■ Belfast

The Belfast shipyard of Harland & Wolff is a
pale shadow of the industrial giant that employed
25,000 men and launched *Titanic* in 1912. But
Titanic's slipways are still to be seen, as are the
enormous yellow cranes Samson (built in 1974) and
Goliath (1969), symbols of Belfast. See all this and
more of the dockyards on one of the Lagan Boat
Company's 'Titanic Tours'.

▶ *Lagan Boat Company, Donegall Quay*
✆ *028 9033 0844;* **www.laganboatcompany.com**

■ Carrick-a-Rede, Co. Antrim

The most famous bridge in Northern Ireland is also
the flimsiest, a cat's-cradle of ropes and planking that
pitches and sways as you cross it 100 feet above the
sea. In times past, local fishermen would sling Carrick-
a-Rede rope bridge each spring between the Ballintoy
cliffs and the rock 60 feet offshore from which they

would spread their salmon nets. The rock is called
Carrick-a-Rede, 'the rock in the roadway', because
it forms an obstacle in the main tideway, forcing the
salmon to turn aside and seek the alternative channel
where fisherman would spread their nets. The salmon
fishery has been redundant for a few years, but the
bridge is still slung each spring and dismantled each
autumn.

🚗 *Off B15, 5 miles west of Ballycastle*
(Giant's Causeway 10 mins)
▶ *NTNI* ✆ *028 2073 1582 (North Antrim office)*

■ Carrickfergus Castle, Co. Antrim

With its forbidding grey walls sheltering a Norman
keep almost 100 feet tall, Carrickfergus Castle stands
over its harbour at the entrance to Belfast Lough as if
daring any rash invader to try to approach the city.

🚗 *On A2 in Carrickfergus*
▶ *EHSNI* ✆ *028 9335 1273*

■ Castle Ward, Co. Down

This is a most extraordinary building, its bizarre
marriage of architectural styles the result of a fine
display of eighteenth-century marital stubbornness.
Bernard Ward wanted tastefully restrained classicism
and got his way with the front of the house, inside and
out; his wife, Lady Anne, insisted on exuberant Gothic,
and modelled the back part to suit herself.

🚗 *7 miles north-east of Downpatrick on A25*
▶ *NTNI* ✆ *028 4488 1204*

■ Cushendun, Co. Antrim

Arts and Crafts cottages, white-painted under grey
slated roofs, are the keynote of this charming little
village at the foot of Glendun. It was designed between
1912 and 1923 for landowner Robert McNeill by the
architect of Portmeirion in North Wales, Clough
Williams-Ellis (see page 148, **Places of Interest**).

🚗 *On B92, off A2 north of Cushendall*

■ Londonderry (Derry City), Co. Derry

Derry is a very enjoyable, lively little city, its central
part surrounded by the finest set of city walls in
Ireland. They were built from 1613 to 1618 by
London trade guilds that had been 'planted' in the
city to oversee the establishment of profitable trade
and the upholding of Protestantism. A walk around

Northern Ireland:
Carlingford Lough to Lough Foyle
BETWEEN A ROCK AND A HARD PLACE

the Walls of Derry is a scenic and cultural 'must'.

▶ TIC ☎ 028 7126 7284

■ Downhill, Co. Derry

On the cliffs above Castlerock the remains of the once-great estate of Downhill – the ruins of Downhill palace, its walled garden, and the domed Mussenden Temple on the cliff edge – speak clearly of the extravagance and eccentricities of the larger-than-life Frederick Hervey (1730–1803), 4th Earl of Bristol and Protestant Bishop of Londonderry. Stories tell of the red-blooded Hervey installing one of his mistresses in the temple. What is certainly true is that he was a generous and ecumenically minded bishop, who allowed the local Catholic priest to say Mass in the temple at a time of widespread religious intolerance.

🚗 5 miles from Coleraine on A2

▶ NTNI ☎ 028 7084 8728

■ Dunluce Castle, Co. Antrim

Dunluce Castle stands in magnificent ruin on the cliffs. Sorley Boy MacDonnell recaptured the castle from the English in 1584 with the help of fighters who he'd had pulled up the sheer cliffs in baskets. A storm in 1639 sent the castle kitchens toppling into the sea, killing several cooks. After the Battle of the Boyne in 1690, the MacDonnells, supporters of the defeated King James II, were imprisoned and Dunluce was abandoned.

🚗 On A2 between Bushmills and Portrush

▶ EHSNI ☎ 028 2073 1938

■ Giant's Causeway, Co. Antrim

Thirty-seven thousand hexagonal basalt stumps form the grand promontory of the Giant's Causeway that slopes into the sea from the cliffs near Bushmills. Plans for a visitor centre worthy of a UNESCO World Heritage Site have been bogged down ever since the previous one burned down in 2000. The present visitor centre, a stopgap, is barely adequate. Independent travellers can bypass it by approaching via the Causeway Coast Path (see **Activities, Walking**, above).

🚗 On B146, well signposted from Bushmills

▶ NTNI ☎ 028 2073 1582 (North Antrim office)

▶ Visitor Centre ☎ 028 2073 1855

■ Kearney, Co. Down

A perfect example of what the National Trust does so well – the whitewashed fishermen's houses of Kearney, and a beautifully kept path around unspoiled cliffs and beaches at the southern point of the Ards Peninsula.

🚗 Follow road signs from Portaferry

▶ NTNI ☎ 028 4488 1411/1668

■ Kilclief Castle, Co. Down

The fifteenth-century tower house of Kilclief was built by the Bishop of Down, John Cely. Another of Northern Ireland's hot-blooded clergymen, he was defrocked in 1441 after it was discovered that he had installed his lover, Lettice Savage – a married woman – in his tower.

🚗 On A2 Strangford–Ardglass road

▶ EHSNI ☎ 028 9181 1491

■ Larne, Co. Antrim

These days the port of Larne connects Belfast by ferry with Fleetwood in Lancashire and with the south-west Scottish ports of Cairnryan and Troon. Larne Harbour has a niche in Irish political history, for it was here in April 1914 that loyalist activists, backed by the Ulster Unionist party, illegally landed thousands of rifles and tons of ammunition, ratcheting up the tension between loyalists and republicans that would lead to the Easter Rising of 1916 and the partition of Northern and Southern Ireland.

■ Lecale Peninsula, Co. Down

Lecale is the blunt-nosed bulge of land east of Downpatrick, with a fine 22-mile coast drive taking in such features as Kilclief Castle (see above), Ardglass Harbour defended by towers and forts, and the promontory of St John's Point with its black-and-yellow lighthouse and ruined tenth-century chapel.

▶ Downpatrick TIC ☎ 028 4461 2233

■ Strangford Lough, Co. Down

Strangford Lough is one of the most fascinating places in Northern Ireland, a tidal inlet 23 miles long into which the sea pours twice daily through the narrow gap that separates the twin ferry villages of Strangford and Portaferry. Birds of coast and sea haunt the lough; you can watch them from the boardwalks and hides at Castle Espie Wildfowl and Wetlands Centre (see

Activities, Birdwatching, above). Strangford Lough's tidal islands were refuges for early Christian hermits such as the fifth-century St Mochaoi of Nendrum monastery on Mahee Island (who once had St Patrick as a visiting preacher), and the lough shores attracted later holy men like the monks of Grey Abbey. Secular men built here for the view, as was the case with the Marquis of Londonderry and his beautiful eighteenth-century country house called Mount Stewart; the lovely gardens and grounds here were laid out by Edith, Lady Londonderry, in the 1920s.

🚗 *Strangford Lough Wildlife Scheme: Castle Ward, near Strangford*
NTNI ☎ 028 4488 1411/1668
🚗 *Nendrum Monastery, Mahee Island: signposted off A22 immediately south of Comber*
EHSNI ☎ 028 9181 1491
🚗 *Grey Abbey: Church Street, Greyabbey, on A20*
EHSNI ☎ 028 9054 6552
🚗 *Mount Stewart: on A20, 5 miles south-east of Newtownards*
NTNI ☎ 028 4278 8387

RESORTS

■ Ballycastle, Co. Antrim
Ballycastle is a small pleasant town near the Giant's Causeway on the Antrim Coast, with one great claim to fame: Ould Lammas Fair, the great annual spree in late August that sees the town filled with holidaymakers, stallholders, travellers and horses. That's when everyone eats dulse (edible seaweed collected locally) and yellowman toffee, Ballycastle's twin specialities.
▸ *TIC ☎ 028 2076 2024*

■ Newcastle, Co. Down
Newcastle occupies a prime position above a sandy beach, with the Mountains of Mourne pressing dramatically in at the back of the town. This is very much a small-scale, traditional resort with plenty of beach activity by day and not too much action at night.
▸ *TIC ☎ 028 4372 2222*

■ Portrush, Co. Antrim
Portrush is a big, vibrant resort with a lively air and plenty to do – attractions include Barry's Amusement

Park, Waterworld swimming centre, a Countryside Centre with suggestions for what to do along the Antrim coast, and three really fine swimming beaches to choose from, each with coveted Blue Flag status.
▸ *TIC ☎ 028 7082 3333 (summer only)*

■ Portstewart, Co. Derry
Portstewart is Portrush's rather quieter and more sober older brother, a laid-back Victorian resort with a superb beach just around the corner. Golfers flock to Portstewart for its three golf courses. Each May, things get a little rowdier when the North West 200 motorcycle race fills the streets as the bikes zoom between Portstewart, Portrush and Coleraine.
▸ *TIC ☎ 028 7083 2286*

Useful Websites
www.ehsni.gov.uk
www.ntni.org.uk
www.goodbeachguide.co.uk
www.ulsterwildlifetrust.org
www.rspb.org.uk
www.wwt.org.uk
www.bbc.co.uk/coast

Northern Ireland: Carlingford Lough to Lough Foyle
BETWEEN A ROCK AND A HARD PLACE

The Solway Firth to
the Isle of Skye
THE BATTLEGROUND COAST

All tourist information ☎ 0845 2255121;
www.visitscotland.com

ACTIVITIES

■ Birdwatching

Whether it's sea eagles on the Isle of Rhum or golden eagles in Knoydart, the west coast of Scotland will give you every chance to see magnificent birds. There are puffins and razorbills on the cliffs of the Mull of Galloway, Greenland white-fronted geese in the Islay peat bogs, barnacle geese on the Solway merses at Caerlaverock (WWT reserve) and corncrakes in the grasses of Coll and North Uist (RSPB reserves). In all, the RSPB maintains seven reserves on the west coast and islands, and these are good places to start.

■ Mountaineering and walking

Walking and mountaineering are glorious all along this coast. There are few official rights of way, but you are welcome to walk virtually anywhere. Long-distance paths include the Isle of Arran Coastal Way (65 miles), the West Island Way through the Isle of Bute (26 miles), and the Cowal Way through southern Argyllshire (47 miles). The Walking Wild website has hundreds of walk routes and ideas throughout the area.

▶ **www.mountaineering-scotland.org.uk**
▶ **www.walkingwild.com**

CASTLES

■ Caerlaverock, Dumfries and Galloway

The Maxwells were a formidable border family, always fussing and feuding with their neighbours, and it was they who built Caerlaverock Castle in the wild marshy country of the Solway Firth. The castle was designed on a triangular plan, unique in Scotland, and surrounded by a double moat. Captured by Edward I in 1300, it saw three turbulent centuries before a fine gentleman's residence was built inside the courtyard, signalling the arrival of quieter times on the Scottish border.

🚗 *8 miles south-east of Dumfries on B725*
▶ *HS* ☎ *01387 770244*

■ Castle Tioram, Highland

The fourteenth-century Castle Tioram was built by the Macdonalds in a highly romantic but also militarily logical location, in Loch Moidart on a tidal island only reachable at low tide. It has stood in various states of picturesque dilapidation since 1715, when Allan of Clanranald had it burned to prevent enemies taking it over while he was away supporting the Old Pretender in the first Jacobite Rising.

🚗 *Near Acharacle on A861*

■ Culzean Castle, Ayrshire

Perched in a striking position on the edge of the Ayrshire cliffs, the medieval castle of Culzean was redesigned by Robert Adam in the late eighteenth century as a romantic mansion. The interior has been furnished in superb Georgian style; its centrepiece is Adam's grand and graceful oval staircase.

🚗 *12 miles south of Ayr, on A719*
▶ *NTS* ☎ *01655 884455*

ISLANDS

🚢 Routes from **www.calmac.co.uk/islands.html**
✈ Services from **www.hial.co.uk**
Outer Hebrides islands information:
www.visithebrides.com

■ Arran, Ayrshire

A 'Scotland in miniature', Arran has fine hill walking, golf courses galore, the low-key seaside resort of Brodick with its sixteenth-century castle (NTS), and the 2868-foot mini-mountain of Goat Fell to climb for stunning views over the Firth of Clyde.

🚢 *From Ardrossan or Claonaig*
▶ *Ayrshire and Arran Tourist Board, Prestwick*
☎ *01292 678100;* **www.ayrshire-arran.com**

■ Barra, Outer Hebrides

Barra lays magic on you from the moment you arrive – either on a ferry as you pass Kisimul Castle (HS) rising like a fairytale fortress on its rock in Castlebay Harbour, or in an aeroplane that touches down not on an airfield but on the broad white cockleshell sands of Traigh Mhór, the 'Great Beach'. From Barra's one circular road, rough tracks lead up and over the knobby back of the island.

🚢 *From Oban or South Uist*
✈ *From Glasgow or Benbecula*
▶ *Barra Heritage and Cultural Centre* ☎ *01871 810413*
▶ **www.isleofbarra.com**

■ Bute, Argyllshire

Glasgow's 'home island', Bute lies in the mouth of the Firth of Clyde, conveniently close to the capital. Though paddle-steamers no longer take Glaswegians 'doon th' watter' in vast numbers, Bute's Victorian resort of Rothesay still does good holiday business. Mount Stuart, south of Rothesay, is a wonderful Gothic extravaganza of a house, built by Cardiff coal mogul the 3rd Marquess of Bute in the 1870s.

⛴ *From Wemyss Bay or Colintraive*

▸ *Mount Stuart Visitor Centre*
(Mon/Wed/Fri/Sat/Sun) ☏ *01700 505808*

▸ **www.isle-of-bute.com**

■ Coll, Inner Hebrides

Grey volcanic rock shows through Coll's thin covering of heather and grass. This is a bleak island, yet one whose entire southern end is carefully managed as an RSPB reserve to safeguard the corncrake, a small brown bird whose rarity outweighs its nondescript appearance and grating call. Dr Samuel Johnson and his friend and biographer James Boswell were entertained royally on Coll by its heroic young laird, Donald Maclean, when a storm drove their boat into the island during their grand tour of western Scotland in 1773 – an adventure recounted in Johnson and Boswell's joint book, *A Journey to the Western Isles of Scotland/A Journal of a Tour to the Hebrides*.

⛴ *From Oban or Tiree*

▸ **www.isleofcoll.org**

■ Eigg, Muck and Rhum, Inner Hebrides

Known as the 'Cocktail Isles', these three neighbouring islands have widely differing characters. The islanders of Eigg, disillusioned with the rule of a succession of increasingly neglectful private owners, set up the Isle of Eigg Heritage Trust, which bought the island in 1997. Eigg boasts a spectacular geology encompassing the squeaky quartz grains of Singing Sands beach, a great curtain of basalt cliffs above Cleadale, and the 1292-foot Sgurr peak with its columns of pitchstone lava. Tiny, low-lying Muck is owned and farmed by the MacEwen family, who run an excellent guesthouse at Port Mór. Rhum, by contrast, consists of 26,000 acres of high mountain and wild moorland run as a nature reserve by Scottish Natural Heritage. Watch red deer, otters and sea eagles, or enjoy a look round the red sandstone Kinloch Castle where time has stood still since the Edwardian era.

⛴ *From Mallaig*

▸ **www.road-to-the-isles.org.uk**

■ Harris, Outer Hebrides

Harris is not really an island in its own right, being connected by land to its northerly neighbour of Lewis, but it has an entirely different character, with harshly naked mountains of gneiss dominating the landscape. The capital village of Tarbert straddles a 900-foot-wide isthmus that joins north and south Harris. The island's famous tweed is still handwoven by the islanders, its credibility protected by the Harris Tweed Act of 1993 and by the Orb symbol of authenticity.

⛴ *From Uig or Berneray*

▸ **www.harristweed.com**

■ Iona, Inner Hebrides (NTS)

Iona has seen hermits, kings and pilgrims come and go for nearly 1500 years, ever since the Irish saint Columba steered his boat into Port a' Churaich, the 'harbour of the coracle', in 563AD. On the tiny island off the south-west tip of Mull, Columba founded a Celtic church, whose flame burned brightly for a thousand years. In the mid-twentieth century, the ecumenical Iona Community restored the ruined abbey. The Community operates the hospitable MacLeod Centre there today. The nearby island museum displays the graveslabs of nearly 50 Scottish kings.

⛴ *From Fionnphort, Mull*

▸ **www.isle-of-iona.com**

■ Islay, Inner Hebrides

Islay is the most south-westerly of the Hebridean islands, and traditional seat of the Macdonald clan, Lords of the Isles. You can visit the site of their court on an islet in Loch Finlaggan, admire the 1200-year-old sculptures of Kildalton High Cross and take a tour round one of half a dozen distilleries producing the distinctive peat-flavoured Islay malt whiskies. Or just walk down to the seabird-haunted cliffs of the Mull of Oa Peninsula to view the Antrim cliffs in Northern Ireland a few miles away across the sea.

🛳 *From Kennacraig, Kintyre*

✈ *From Glasgow*

▶ **www.islay.co.uk**

■ **Jura, Inner Hebrides**

Jura is Islay's north-easterly neighbour, an island with a roadless 50-mile west coast and the three bare quartzite peaks of the Paps of Jura. Craighouse on the east side is the only settlement of any size. At Barnhill, 20 miles up the coast from Craighouse, George Orwell wrote *1984* from 1947 to 1948.

🛳 *From Islay*

▶ **www.juradevelopment.co.uk**

■ **Lewis, Outer Hebrides**

Lewis is the most northerly and by far the biggest island in the Outer Hebrides, a 40-mile stretch of peat bog and tiny lochs with its capital, Stornoway, the only town. Lewis is also the windiest place in the islands; hence the proposal for a wind farm of 234 turbines, each of them over 450 feet tall, plus attendant roads, pylons and cables, generating 702 megawatts, enough to serve almost half a million homes. Set against that are the hard-to-quantify assets of rare and easily displaced birds, uncluttered landscapes that incorporate ancient monuments such as the Callanish stone circle, and a wide empty horizon to contemplate.

🛳 *From Ullapool*

✈ *From Glasgow, Edinburgh, Benbecula, Barra, Inverness*

▶ **www.isle-of-lewis.com**

■ **Mull, Inner Hebrides**

Mull is a great ragged layer-cake of basalt lying opposite the port of Oban. Tobermory is the chief town, and there are a couple of other small settlements. Otherwise the island is mostly basalt ledges and cliffs, harshly shaped mountains and superbly lonely coasts. Red deer, otters, sea eagles and golden eagles thrive here, and it's a good spot for watching dolphins and minke whales, basking sharks and porpoise.

🛳 *From Oban, Kilchoan or Lochaline*

▶ **www.isle.of.mull.com**

■ **North Uist and South Uist, Outer Hebrides**

These two islands, separated by Benbecula, have roughly the same topography: sharply rising ground sweeping up into bleak mountains on the east, and on the Atlantic side, beautiful beaches of white sand backed by shell-enriched grassy swards called machair, which carry thick carpets of flowers.

🛳 *North Uist from Uig or Berneray*

🛳 *South Uist from Oban or Barra*

▶ **www.uistonline.com**

■ **Rockall**

A bleak tooth of weather-beaten and wave-washed Atlantic Ocean rock some 300 miles from Britain at 57 35' N, 13 48' W, Rockall is nevertheless UK territory and mentioned in the shipping forecast. Its online newspaper, *The Rockall Times*, is required reading.

▶ **www.therockalltimes.co.uk**

■ **Skye, Inner Hebrides**

Skye is the biggest and best known of the Hebridean islands, famed as the place to which Bonnie Prince Charlie and Flora Macdonald fled in 1746 after the Battle of Culloden. Here are the great Black and Red Cuillin Hills, the basalt cliffs of the Quiraing, Dunvegan Castle and the Fairy Flag of the Macleods, Armadale Castle and the Clan Donald Centre. You can stay in the self-catering cottage at Flodigarry where Flora Macdonald raised her children, and visit her grave at Kilmuir nearby.

🚌 *A87 from Kyle of Lockalsh*

▶ **www.skye.co.uk**

■ **Staffa, Inner Hebrides**

It can be a bumpy boat ride out to Staffa, but the little island off Mull is worth the trip. This is a volcanic masterpiece – an extraordinary structure of hexagonal basalt columns topped with a flower-rich sward and pierced with a sea cavern called Fingal's Cave that is the size of a cathedral nave, and inspired Mendelssohn's eponymous overture.

🛳 *From Ulva Ferry* ☎ *01688 500241 or Fionnphort* ☎ *0161 700338, Isle of Mull.*

▶ *NNR managed by NTS*

■ **Tiree, Inner Hebrides**

Tiree and Coll lie close together, but unlike its neighbour, Tiree is no lumpy basalt crag. This is a green and fertile island of pristine beaches, beautiful flowery grasslands and low hills. Even the airstrip is a carpet of wild flowers. Tiree is one of the windiest places in Britain, and storms on the wave-pounded western beaches are spectacular.

🚢 *From Oban or Coll*

✈ *From Glasgow*

▸ **www.scotland-inverness.co.uk/tiree**

NATURAL WORLD

The natural world of Scotland's west coast and islands is sublimely rich with pristine beaches; great cliffs of sandstone that turn to basalt as you go north; mountains rising from coastal glens and island shores; marshes packed with birds along the Solway Firth; and great shingle beds on the Atlantic-facing coasts of the Treshnish islands, Jura, Arran and the Rhinns of Galloway.

PLACES OF INTEREST

■ Firth of Clyde

The Firth of Clyde is a beautiful waterway fringed by hills, its south bank lined with old settlements such as the shipyard town of Greenock and the attractively down-at-heel Victorian resort of Gourock. Today sailing boats parade where the Atlantic convoys of the Second World War would assemble at the mouth of the Clyde.

■ Knoydart, Highland

The Old Forge at Inverie, on the Knoydart peninsula north of Mallaig, is the remotest pub in Britain – officially, as confirmed by *The Guinness Book of Records*. The pub manages to keep stocked with good real ales and serves great locally sourced food. Inverie is a community without road access – you have either to walk in, or get a boat from Mallaig. The village has almost died on several occasions, but incomers determined to make life work there have breathed new vigour into the place.

▸ *The Old Forge* ☎ *01687 462267;*
www.theoldforge.co.uk

■ Loch nan Uamh, Highland

Bonnie Prince Charlie, in high hopes of gaining the throne of Britain, first set foot on the Scottish mainland on 25 July 1745 at Loch nan Uamh, the Loch of the Caves, near Arisaig in South Morar. He left for France 14 months later on 19 September 1746, a bitter fugitive with his dreams in tatters and the clans who had supported him in ruins. A cairn on the hillside marks his leaving place.

■ Logan Botanic Garden, Dumfries and Galloway

In the Walled Garden at Logan, the springtime blooms of rhododendrons, camellias and magnolias give way to spectacular displays of Cape daisies, fuchsia, sages and verbena, not to mention tree ferns and cabbage palms. The Woodland Garden features trees and other plants from South America and Australia.

🚗 *14 miles south of Stranraer on B7065*

▸ *RBGE (Royal Botanic Garden Edinburgh)*

☎ *01776 860231;* **www.rbge.org.uk**

RESORTS

■ Ardrossan, Prestwick and Troon, Ayrshire

Ardrossan is an old-fashioned resort with good sandy beaches (and a hilarious website – **www.geocities.com/lordeglinton**). Prestwick has a very scenic seaside golf course; Troon offers a yacht marina and the three courses of Royal Troon Golf Club.

Useful Websites

www.nts.org.uk
www.snh.org.uk
www.rspb.org.uk/scotland
www.historic-scotland.gov.uk
www.nnr-scotland.org.uk
www.visitscotland.com
www.escapetotheedge.co.uk
www.bbc.co.uk/coast

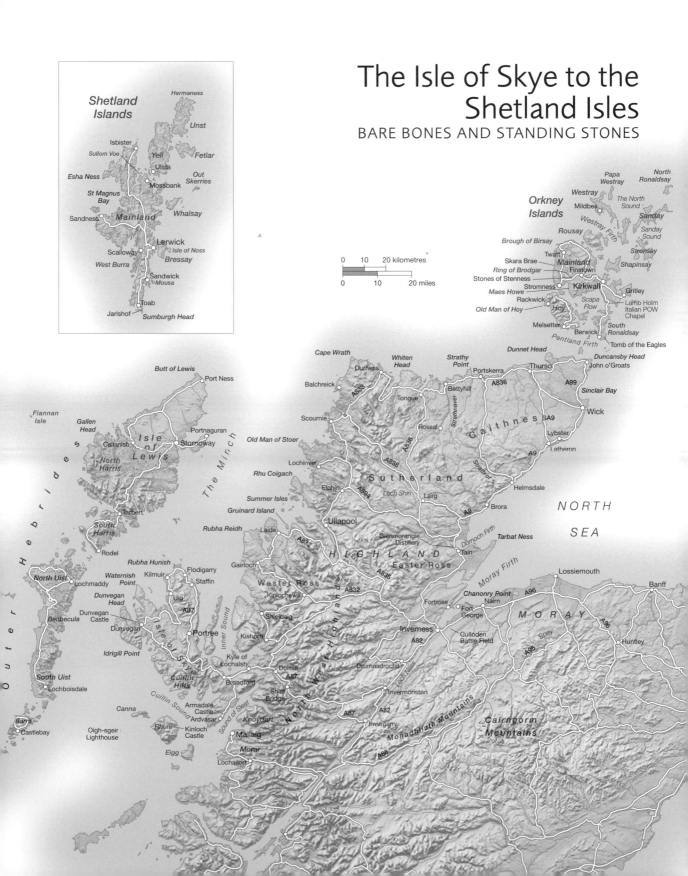

All tourist information ☎ 0845 2255121;
www.visitscotland.com

ACTIVITIES

■ Archaeology

The north of Scotland is rich in Stone Age and Bronze
Age monuments, especially the Orkney archipelago
(see **Islands**, below), which contains the most remarkable collection of prehistoric houses, tombs, standing
stones and defensive structures anywhere in Britain.

■ Birdwatching

The best of northern Scotland's birdwatching tends to
be of seabirds. The Shetland archipelago (see **Islands**,
below) has impressive numbers of guillemot, kittiwake,
fulmar and gannet on the cliffs of the Isle of Noss (NNR),
reached from Bressay by boat, and also on those of the
NNR at Hermaness, the northernmost point of the island
of Unst, where gannet and puffin vie with aggressive
great skuas. The RSPB maintains 17 reserves in Orkney
and Shetland. For birds of passage, the best bet is
lonely Fair Isle, midway between the two archipelagos.

■ Fishing

Fishing is excellent throughout the area. Many of
the mainland lochs offer coarse fishing, while several
wonderful salmon and sea trout rivers such as the
Borgie, Naver and Strathy run to the north coast. The
thousands of lochs in Shetland are full of brown trout.

■ Music

Shetland is famous for the vigour and wildness of its
fiddle music. To catch some great tunes (and join in if
you wish), try The Lounge bar in Lerwick; for dances
and music sessions throughout the islands, ask at Lerwick
Tourist Information Centre.

ISLANDS

■ Flannan Isle

This bleak, remote island 15 miles west of Lewis has one
bizarre claim to fame – the disappearance of all three
of its lighthouse keepers on 14th or 15th December
1900. The mystery is still unexplained, but it was
probably a freak storm wave that washed them away.

■ Gruinard

Like Flannan Isle, Gruinard is famous for one thing –

in 1942 it was the scene of Second World War
biological war-fare experiments with anthrax. The
little island was so grossly contaminated with the
spores of the deadly bacteria that it was closed to
the public until 1990.

▶ *Off A832 between Gairloch and Ullapool*

■ Orkney Archipelago

▶ *Visit Orkney Tourist Information, Kirkwall*
☎ *01856 872856;* **www.visitorkney.com**
Orkney Mainland: 🚢 *From John O'Groats, Scrabster,
Aberdeen;* ✈ *From Aberdeen, Edinburgh, Wick,
Glasgow, Inverness, Sumburgh*
All inhabited Orkney islands: 🚢 *From Orkney Mainland;*
✈ *From Orkney Mainland to Eday, North Ronaldsay,
Papa Westray, Sanday, Stronsay and Westray*

HOY

Hoy lies off the south-west corner of Orkney
Mainland. While visiting the Old Man of Hoy (see
Natural World, Sea stacks, below), make time to
see the Dwarfie Stane, a strange creation 5000 years
old, which incorporates two cramped chambers, too
small for an ordinary-sized person, cut into a huge
block of sandstone.

ORKNEY MAINLAND

Orkney Mainland is the 'capital' island of the
archipelago. Kirkwall (TIC ☎ 01856 872856) is the
chief town and site of the splendid red sandstone
cathedral of St Magnus, founded in the twelfth
century by Rognvald Earl of Orkney in memory of his
murdered uncle Magnus. Stromness is a lively little
seaport to the west of Kirkwall. Mainland is full of
wonderful archaeological sites – some of the best are:
Brough of Birsay Twelfth-century church, a Pictish
stone and some Norse houses on a tidal island off
the north-west corner of Mainland.

▶ *Tide times: contact Kirkwall TIC*

Maes Howe Built around 2700BC, this is the finest
chambered tomb in Europe. You enter the grassy mound
on your knees along a low tunnel, then emerge into the
central chamber of massive, neatly fitted stones, its walls
pierced with three recesses. The doorway of the tomb
is aligned so that the last ray of the setting sun at the
midwinter solstice shines into the heart of Maes Howe.

Runes incised into the stones tell how Hakon the Viking broke into the tomb and took away a treasure.

🚗 *At Tormiston Mill on A965 west of Kirkwall*

☎ *01856 761606*

Ring of Brodgar (sometimes called 'Brogar') A very fine and impressive circle of standing stones – slim blade-like objects, some with their tops cut sharply on the diagonal. The 60 stones were originally erected between 2500 and 2000 BC, and about half still stand.

🚗 *Off B9055 between Finstown and Stromness*

▶ *HS* ☎ *01856 841815*

Skara Brae A village buried in a sand dune some 4000 years ago. The houses have been perfectly preserved with their stone tables, beds and shelves.

🚗 *Off A967 north of Stromness*

▶ *HS* ☎ *01856 841815*

Stones of Stenness Only five stones of this circle, perhaps 500 years older than the Ring of Brodgar, still stand, but they are magnificent – the tallest is almost 20 feet high.

🚗 *Off B9055 near Ring of Brodgar (see above)*

▶ *HS* ☎ *01856 841815*

PAPA WESTRAY

The most northerly of the Orkney islands, and one of the smallest, possesses on its west coast one of the archaeological gems of Orkney – a Stone Age house and its workshop, side by side in the dunes at Knap of Howar. Built some 5500 years ago, these little stone-walled structures are the oldest buildings still standing in northern Europe.

ROUSAY

Rousay lies just north of Mainland. On its southern shore at Midhowe stands the building that houses the breathtaking 'Great Ship of Rousay', sometimes called the Ship of Death. The 'ship', constructed about 3500 BC, is an enormous multiple tomb 100 feet long, with 12 compartments ranged along it in which excavators found the remains of 25 people who had been entombed in crouching positions.

SANDAY

Thin-bodied and sandy, the island of Sanday sprawls towards the north-east of the Orkney archipelago. Quoyness Chambered Cairn is its archaeological jewel,

another great stone room of a tomb buried in a mound almost 5000 years ago.

SOUTH RONALDSAY

At the southern end of the island chain in Scapa Flow (see **Natural World, Natural harbours**, below), South Ronaldsay holds the extraordinary Isbister Chambered Tomb, better known as the Tomb of the Eagles. Excavations revealed the human bones and fragments of around 350 people, and the scattered remains of eight or more white-tailed eagles.

■ **Shetland Archipelago**

▶ *Shetland Islands Tourism, Lerwick* ☎ *01595 693434;* **www.visitshetland.com***;* **www.shetland-heritage.co.uk**

Shetland Mainland: 🚢 *From Aberdeen, Orkney Mainland;* ✈ *From Aberdeen, Edinburgh, Orkney Mainland, Glasgow, Inverness*

All inhabited Shetland islands: 🚢 *From Shetland Mainland;* ✈ *From Shetland Mainland to Fair Isle, Foula, Out Skerries, Papa Stour*

FAIR ISLE

Fair Isle lies between Shetland Mainland and the Orkney archipelago, 25 miles from both. The island is only three miles long and about half that wide; a tiny slip of land famous among birdwatchers for the huge variety of birds that use Fair Isle as a staging post on their migratory journeys. The Fair Isle Bird Observatory has recorded almost 350 species since its 1948 inception. The well-known Fair Isle knitting is also still produced on the island – most of it machine-made these days, but some hand-knitted garments might be available for lucky purchasers with deep pockets. The 70-odd islanders are extremely hospitable, and island dances and celebrations are memorable affairs.

▶ *NTS;* **www.fairisle.org.uk**

FETLAR

Fetlar lies just east of Yell. It's a rugged island with a small population of humans and a large one of birds, including red-throated divers, whimbrels, golden plovers, black guillemots and almost all the UK population of red-necked phalaropes – hence the presence of an RSPB reserve.

▶ *RSPB* ☎ *01957 693434*

The Isle of Skye to the Shetland Isles

BARE BONES AND STANDING STONES

FOULA

The population of Foula has diminished to not much more than 30, but those who remain are determined to stick to their lonely crofting way of life (and their observance of the Julian calendar, eg. Christmas Day on 6 January and New Year's Eve on 13 January) on this tiny island 20 miles west of Shetland Mainland.

▶ **www.lonely-isles.com**

SHETLAND MAINLAND

Shetland's chief island stretches long and thin to north and south, its sides so deeply indented by the wild weather and seas of the Atlantic that although the island is 55 miles long, nowhere lies more than three miles from the sea. The landscape is virtually treeless, a mosaic of peat bog, loch and dark rock that is moody but compelling. Some of the principal attractions are:

Jarlshof An extraordinary site at the southern tip of Mainland, where Bronze Age huts, Iron Age wheelhouses, Norse longhouses, medieval farms and lordly dwellings lie piled together in an exotic archaeological sandwich.

🚗 *Off A970 near Sumburgh Airport*

▶ *HS* ☎ *01950 460112*

▶ **www.shetland-museum.org.uk**

Lerwick Shetland's vigorous, windswept and salty little capital town, with a lively and hardworking waterfront and a maze of narrow, steep lanes behind, really comes into its own on the last Tuesday of each January, when the feast of Up Helly Aa sees fully costumed Norsemen take over the town. They drag with them a full-size longship, which they burn with great ceremony at nightfall before embarking on a long night of drinking, dancing and wild charades.

Mousa Broch By far the best surviving example of one of these distinctive Iron Age defensive towers, the broch on the islet of Mousa stands 40 feet tall, its hollow walls concealing flights of stairs up to the ramparts.

🚢 *From Sandwich*

▶ *HS* ☎ *0131 6688800*

Scalloway Shetland's capital in former times is a neat little fishing port overlooked by the fine grim 400-year-old stronghold of Earl Patrick Stewart's castle. The town museum has a good display on Scalloway's role as the base of operations of the 'Shetland Bus', a fleet of fishing boats that ran arms, agents and supplies across the North Sea to the Norwegian Resistance during the Second World War.

▶ *Scalloway Museum* ☎ *01595 880783*

Sullom Voe Oil Terminal When the Brent oilfield was discovered under the North Sea 100 miles north-east of Shetland in 1972, the Shetland Island Council acted wisely in buying up the land around the wide deep-water inlet of Sullom Voe for the purpose of building a huge oil terminal there. The SIC leases the land to the oil companies and runs the Port of Sullom Voe, a strange sight – a vast industrial concern in a bleak, empty landscape.

UNST

The most northerly island in Britain, Unst's north–south geography has produced a landscape that undulates in parallel lines. The island is rich in minerals and has been quarried and mined for roadstone, iron chromite, talc and chromium, while there has been sporadic talk of platinum and gold mining. But most of this industry is dead or dormant. Walking the final three miles north, you reach the cliffs of Hermaness bird reserve, from where the view northwards is over a group of sharply canted rock stacks, musically named Vesta Skerry, Rumblings, Tipta Skerry and Muckle Flugga, to the rounded blob of Out Stack, the final full stop to the British Isles. Next point north is the Arctic Circle.

YELL

Sea otters, wild flowers, seabirds and beautiful deserted beaches are features of Yell, but to find them you have to leave the main road through the rectangular island that forms a stepping stone between Mainland and Unst. The road crosses interminable peat moors, and Yell from this perspective can seem the bleakest place on earths.

NATURAL WORLD

■Cliffs

With some of Britain's oldest and hardest rocks as its foundations, the north of Scotland possesses several mighty sections of cliff. The towering cliffs of pink gneiss and dusky sandstone at Cape Wrath are particularly symbolic, for the intransigence of their name (actually a Norse word for 'turning point') as much as for their location at the point where the mainland coast turns from the crashing waves of the Atlantic towards those of the North Sea.

■ Natural harbours

Scapa Flow forms the largest natural harbour in Britain, sheltered on the north by Orkney Mainland and protected by a semi-circle of smaller islands: Hoy, Flotta, Burray and South Ronaldsay. During the First World War, it was the British Grand Fleet's northern anchorage, and the scene on 21 June 1919 of the scuttling of the interned German High Seas Fleet – 8 of the 74 ships still lie on the bottom. On 14 October 1939, Kapitänleutnant Günther Prien slipped his submarine U-47 through a gap between Lamb Holm islet and Mainland into Scapa Flow, and torpedoed the battleship HMS *Royal Oak* with the loss of 833 lives. Subsequently the Churchill Barrier causeways were built between the easterly islands to seal up that means of access to Scapa Flow. The Italian prisoners of POW Camp 60 who were put to work building the barriers made something of their own, too – a beautiful little chapel, constructed of two old Nissen huts and whatever scrap materials they could find, which still stands on Lamb Holm.

▶ **www.scapaflow.co.uk**

■ Sea stacks

The Old Man of Hoy, a tremendous sea stack of red sandstone rising from a granite base off the north-west corner of the Orkney island of Hoy, stands 450 feet tall. One day the sea will claim him; meanwhile he continues to fascinate photographers, sailors and rock climbers.

PLACES OF INTEREST

■ Bettyhill, Sutherland

Bettyhill, on mainland Scotland's extreme north coast, is an early nineteenth-century estate village steeped in Highland history. It was built on the orders of Elizabeth, Countess of Sutherland, to house the people of Rosal, a village in the inland glen of Strathnaver (see below), whose population the Duke of Sutherland had

had evicted in order to make way for more profitable sheep. Bettyhill's Strathnaver Museum tells the story of the Clearances in Sutherland.

🚗 *On A836 west of Thurso*

▶ *Strathnaver Museum* 📞 *01641 521418;*
www.strathnaver.org

■ Duncansby Head, Caithness

A couple of miles beyond John O'Groats, this is 'Outermost Gaeldom', as the writer John Hillaby put it after walking through Britain. These dark kittiwake-haunted cliffs are the furthest point from Land's End.

■ John O'Groats, Caithness

John O'Groats, however, is where most folk stop, to buy a souvenir and be photographed beside the signpost.

■ Strathnaver, Sutherland

Strathnaver was just one of the glens on the 1.5 million-acre estate of the Duke of Sutherland, where the local people were turned out of their homes and off the land to make way for sheep. But Strathnaver had the stonemason Donald Macleod of Rosal to record the savagery and misery of the Clearings, in which he counted 250 houses set ablaze. There is a memorial at Rosal, some visitor interpretation at the Clearance villages of Achanlochy and Dunvidon, and poignant ruins above Loch Naver to explore at Grumbeg.

🚗 *Off B871, B873 north of Bettyhill*

Useful Websites

www.nts.org.uk
www.snh.org.uk
www.historic-scotland.gov.uk
www.nnr-scotland.org.uk
www.visitscotland.com
www.calmac.co.uk
www.undiscoveredscotland.co.uk
www.bbc.co.uk/coast

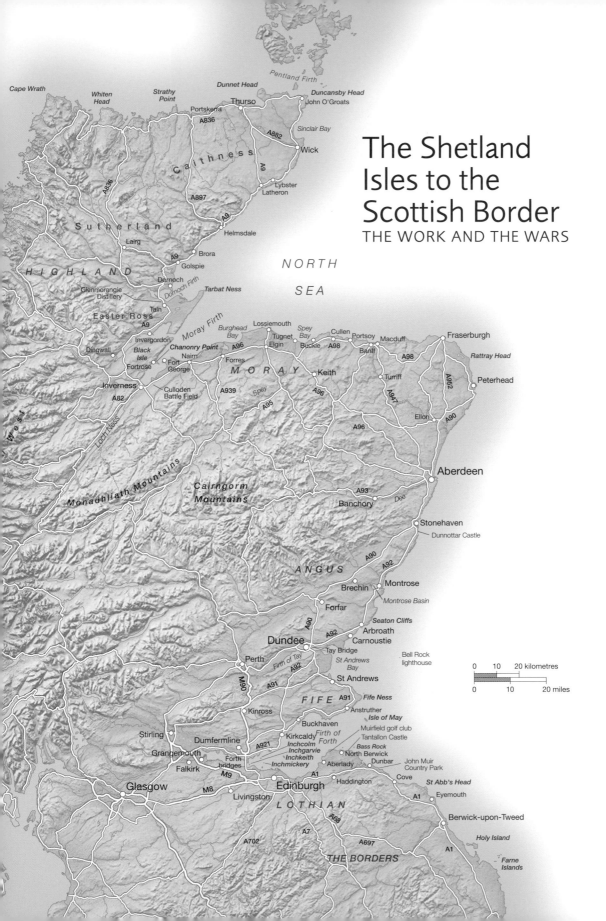

The Shetland Isles to the Scottish Border
THE WORK AND THE WARS

Cape Wrath
Whiten Head
Strathy Point
Dunnet Head
Pentland Firth
Duncansby Head
John O'Groats
Thurso
Portskerra
A836
Sinclair Bay
A882
Wick
Caithness
A9
Lybster
Latheron
A897
A9
Helmsdale

NORTH
SEA

Sutherland
Lairg
A9
Brora
Golspie
HIGHLAND
Dornoch
Glenmorangie Distillery
Dornoch Firth
Tarbat Ness
Easter Ross
Tain
A9
Invergordon
Dingwall
Black Isle
Chanonry Point
Fort George
Nairn
A96
Forres
Burghead Bay
Lossiemouth
Spey Bay
Cullen
Portsoy
Macduff
Fraserburgh
Tugnet
Elgin
Buckie
A98
Banff
A98
Rattray Head
Fortrose
Inverness
A82
Culloden Battle Field
A939
Spey
Keith
MORAY
A96
Turriff
A947
A952
Peterhead
A95
Loch Ness
West
Monadhliath Mountains
Cairngorm Mountains
A96
Ellon
A90

Aberdeen
A93
Banchory
Dee
Stonehaven
Dunnottar Castle
A90
A92
ANGUS
Brechin
Montrose
Montrose Basin
Forfar
Seaton Cliffs
A90
A92
Arbroath
Carnoustie
Dundee
Tay Bridge
Bell Rock lighthouse
Perth
Firth of Tay
St Andrews Bay
A92
M90
A91
St Andrews
FIFE
A91
Fife Ness
Kinross
Anstruther
Isle of May
Buckhaven
Muirfield golf club
Stirling
Dumfermline
Kirkcaldy
Firth of Forth
Tantallon Castle
Grangemouth
A921
Inchcolm
Inchgarvie
Inchkeith
Bass Rock
North Berwick
Falkirk
Forth bridges
Inchmickery
Aberlady
Dunbar
John Muir Country Park
M9
Cove
M8
A1
Haddington
St Abb's Head
Glasgow
Livingston
Edinburgh
Eyemouth
A1
LOTHIAN
A1
A702
A7
A68
Berwick-upon-Tweed
A697
A1
Holy Island
THE BORDERS
Farne Islands

0   10   20 kilometres
0   10   20 miles

All tourist information 📞 0845 2255121;
www.visitscotland.com

ACTIVITIES

■ Birdwatching

There is fine birdwatching for seabird enthusiasts all along Scotland's east coast, especially on the northern cliffs and on the Isle of May (puffins, Arctic terns, razorbills, guillemots) and Bass Rock (gannets). Montrose Basin (see **Natural World, Estuaries**, below) receives internationally important numbers of pink-footed geese, knot and redshank, while Aberlady Bay on the south side of the Firth of Forth also plays host to many thousands of overwintering pinkfeet, and to grey plover and sanderling.

▶ *Montrose Basin, Angus:* **www.swt.org.uk**
▶ *Isle of May, Firth of Forth: see* **Islands**, *below*
▶ *Bass Rock, Firth of Forth: see* **Rocks**, *below*
▶ *Aberlady Bay, East Lothian:*
www.undiscoveredscotland.co.uk

■ Golf

Good golf courses abound in the region. Carnoustie in Angus and Muirfield in East Lothian are just two of the championship courses. But pride of place goes to Fife and the Royal and Ancient Golf Club of St Andrews, the 'Home of Golf', where the world's golfers come to play a ritual round on the Old Course.

▶ *Royal and Ancient Golf Club, St Andrews*
📞 **01334 460000; www.randa.org**
▶ *British Golf Museum, St Andrews* 📞 *01334 460046;*
www.britishgolfmuseum.co.uk

■ Sea-watching

Chanonry Point, north of Inverness near Fortrose, and the cliffs along the Moray Firth are good for sightings of bottle-nosed and common dolphins and harbour porpoise, while further north in Caithness, headlands such as the one at Lybster provide excellent opportunities for spotting orca (killer whale) and minke whale, along with Atlantic white-sided dolphin and Risso's dolphin (grey grampus).

CASTLES

■ Dunnottar, Aberdeenshire

The tall walls, gables and pinnacles of Dunnottar Castle loom up in an impossibly romantic location: a sheer-sided rocky promontory sticking out into the sea a mile south of Stonehaven. The late fourteenth- and fifteenth-century castle ruins and later dwellings that we see today are founded on a succession of strongholds that go back to unrecorded time. In 1685, in an act of savage cruelty, 167 Covenanters or religious dissenters were locked in a dungeon here for two months. Those that survived starvation, disease and bloody retribution for attempting to escape were then transported.

🚗 *Off A92, 1 mile south of Stonehaven*
📞 *01569 762173*

■ Tantallon, East Lothian

The broken but still mightily impressive walls of Tantallon Castle overlook Bass Rock from their clifftop on the south side of the Firth of Forth. Great red curtain walls and the remains of two towers and a Great Hall are what is left of a fourteenth-century Douglas stronghold, battered by Oliver Cromwell's troops in 1651 and abandoned in magnificent ruin.

🚗 *Off A198, 3 miles east of North Berwick*
▶ *HS* 📞 *01620 892727*

ISLANDS

■ Inchcolm

Inchcolm Abbey was built on its tiny Firth of Forth island as an act of thanksgiving by King Alexander I, who was entertained by the hermit of Inchcolm for three days in 1123 after being driven to shelter there in a storm. The abbey with its vaulted monastic buildings and great church dominates the island, across which there are stunning views from the roof of the church tower.

🚢 *From South Queensferry* 📞 *0131 331 4857;*
www.maidoftheforth.co.uk
▶ *HS* 📞 *01383 823332*

■ Isle of May

The Isle of May can be hard to reach; it lies an hour's boat ride from Anstruther Harbour, and landing is only feasible at certain states of weather and tide. Once ashore, you are in a twitcher's paradise populated by Arctic terns (spectacularly aggressive in the breeding season), razorbills and guillemots, black-backed gulls and kittiwakes, and up to 70,000 pairs of puffins.

🛥 *From Anstruther* ✆ *01333 310103;*

www.isleofmayferry.com

▸ *National Nature Reserve run by SNH*
✆ *01334 654038*

NATURAL WORLD

■ Cliffs

There are fine cliffs from Duncansby Head southwards, and more along the Moray coast and down the eastern flank of Berwickshire around St Abb's Head. Seaton Cliffs near Arbroath on the Angus coast are of red sandstone so soft they have been sculpted by wind and sea into caves, arches, hollows and sea stacks. A three-mile nature trail threads through this remarkable scenery.

▸ *Seaton Cliffs lie just north of Arbroath*
▸ *Nature Trail leaflet guide from Arbroath TIC* ✆ *01241 872609 or Montrose Basin Wildlife Centre*
✆ *01674 676336*

■ Coast park

John Muir Country Park was established to honour Scotland's pioneer conservationist, who was born in Dunbar in 1838 and emigrated to North America at the age of eleven. Muir founded America's national parks, but is little known on this side of the Atlantic. In its 1800 acres of East Lothian coastal country you'll find clifftop trails, the sands of Belhaven Bay and stretches of estuary, marsh and woodland.

🚗 *A198 west of Dunbar* ✆ *01368 829917*

■ Estuaries

FIRTH OF FORTH

The Firth of Forth cuts deeply into the south-east Scottish coastline as its shores narrow inland past Edinburgh to reach the road bridge of 1964 and the famous rail bridge of 1890 with its three great cantilever structures. Several small islands dot the waters of the Firth, including the Isle of May and Inchcolm (see **Islands**, above) and Bass Rock (see **Rocks**, below). Other islands include Inchgarvie, Inchmickery and

Inchkeith, all laden with military buildings from the First and Second World Wars. Inchmickery was deliberately made to resemble a battle cruiser to fool German raiders.

FIRTH OF TAY

The Firth of Tay, narrower than the Firth of Forth, cuts between the north coast of the Fife Peninsula and Dundee on the south shore of Angus. The estuary is forever linked with the Tay Bridge Disaster of 28 December 1879, when the central girders of Sir Thomas Bouch's great railway bridge across the Tay collapsed in a storm as a train was crossing them. Engine and carriages plunged into the water, killing all 72 passengers and three crewmen.

MONTROSE BASIN, ANGUS

The National Trust for Scotland and Scottish Wildlife Trust are both involved in the sensitive farming and good environmental management of the Montrose Basin, the broad muddy estuary of the South Esk river. Eels and salmon swim through the basin on their migratory runs, and the wetland is a wintering ground for geese, waders and ducks as well as a summer breeding refuge for sedge warblers, reed buntings and lapwings, and a moulting ground for mute swans.

🚗 *On A92, just south of Montrose*
▸ *NTS; SWT*
▸ *Montrose Basin Wildlife Centre* ✆ *01674 676336;*
www.montrosebasin.org.uk

SPEY BAY, MORAYSHIRE

The River Spey rushes to the sea in the Moray Firth over a wide delta of chattering pebbles. On the shore here at Tugnet, established in an icehouse of 1830 and the buildings of an old fishing station, is the Moray Firth Wildlife Centre and fishing museum. Near the mouth of the Spey stretches the four-mile-long Culbin Bar, whose shingle ridges are thickly grown with heather, crowberry and juniper.

🚗 *Moray Firth Wildlife Centre: signposted from B9014, off A96 between Mosstodloch and Fochabers*
✆ *01343 820339;* **www.mfwc.co.uk**

ROCKS

■ Bass Rock

Off North Berwick, Bass Rock rears 350 feet out of the Firth of Forth, a spectacular volcanic plug whose top glows eerily white with the bodies and effluents of more than 100,000 gannets. You can spy on their activities from the Scottish Seabird Centre in North Berwick with remote-controlled cameras, or run out there on a boat in hopes of landing to spend a few hours among the gannets – an overwhelming sound, sight and stink.

🚤 *From North Berwick (contact Scottish Seabird Centre, North Berwick* ☎ *01620 890202);*

www.seabird.org

■ Bell Rock

Eleven miles south-east of Arbroath the tapering rocket shape of the Bell Rock lighthouse stands on its wickedly disguised reef of rock. The slim, sea-stained tower, built by the great Robert Stevenson from 1807 to 1811, appears to climb straight out of the sea. This is one of the most remote lighthouses in Britain, on one of the deadliest reefs.

▶ **www.bellrock.org.uk**

PLACES OF INTEREST

■ Aberdeen

Strange though it seems for the solemn-looking 'Granite City', Aberdeen was an oil boom town in the 1970s and 1980s, thanks to the newly opened North Sea oilfield offshore. These days things are a little quieter on a Saturday night. The town has plenty of charm, with medieval buildings such as the turreted Provost Skene's House tucked away among the Victorian commercial piles of glittering granite.

■ Anstruther, Fife

You'll hear broad Doric, that old Scots dialect, spoken by the fishermen of Anstruther. 'Auld Ainster' is a fishing town to its seaboot tips, and possesses the excellent Scottish Fishing Museum on the harbour front.

▶ *Scottish Fishing Museum* ☎ *01333 310628;*

www.scotfishmuseum.org

■ Arbroath, Angus

'Arbroath Smokies' – slowly smoked haddocks – have made the town famous, and you can buy them direct from the smokehouses in the old part of town. Nearby stand the jagged sandstone walls and arcades of thirteenth-century Arbroath Abbey.

■ Banff, Aberdeenshire

Banff is a smart town with seventeenth-century buildings from days of prosperity through trade with the Baltic, and fine Georgian architecture paid for by the landowning Duff family who beautified the town as a winter resort and built the splendid baroque mansion of Duff House.

■ Dundee, Angus

Dundee, the ancient seaport on the north shore of the Firth of Tay, was destroyed by Cromwell's men under General Monk in 1651. But Dundee recovered to become Britain's chief whaling port, and the town of 'Jute, Jam and Journalism' – jute to feed the huge Victorian sack mills, jam that poured from Keiller's factories, and journalism in the shape of publishers DC Thompson and their much-loved comics *Beano* and *Dandy*, in which the characters dress and behave as if it's still the 1930s.

■ Eyemouth, Berwickshire

Eyemouth is a vigorous fishing port tucked down into the Berwickshire cliffs, with an excellent small museum where the terrible story of the town's 1881 fishing fleet catastrophe (see page 97) is told.

▶ *Eyemouth Museum* ☎ *01890 750678*

■ Fort George, Inverness

This huge fort at the mouth of the Moray Firth (see pages 90 and 91), built from 1748 to 1769, is like a town enclosed within strong walls. Parts are still used as barracks by the Army today, but you can walk the walls and visit the military museums and old barrack blocks and the magazine where actors bring the harsh lives of eighteenth-century soldiers to life.

🚗 *Off A96 between Nairn and Inverness*

▶ *HS* ☎ *01667 460232*

■ Fraserburgh, Aberdeenshire

Trawlers and Fraserburgh go together like fish and chips, even in a tough era for fishing. You'll find huge modern trawlers in the harbour in front of a neat and attractive town of grey stone buildings, with the Scottish Lighthouse Museum up at the old lighthouse on Kinnaird Head.

▶ *Scottish Lighthouse Museum* ☎ *01346 511022;*

www.lighthousemuseum.co.uk

■ Glenmorangie, Ross-shire

Glenmorangie is one of the classic Highland malt whiskies, and the Glenmorangie Distillery and Visitor Centre sits in a beautiful location on the Dornoch Firth north of Inverness.

▶ ✆ *01862 892477*; **www.glenmorangie.com**

■ Helmsdale, Sutherland

You can go up the strath of Kildonan to pan for gold; or you can just take it easy in little grey stone Helmsdale, a working fishing village with a sturdily constructed harbour. Helmsdale dates mostly from the nineteenth century, when dispossessed farmers cleared from their inland villages at the order of the Duke of Sutherland were resettled here to try to learn to become fishermen.

■ Peterhead, Aberdeenshire

Huge breakwaters enclose Peterhead Bay and shelter the two harbours built by the foremost engineers of their day – the South Harbour in the 1770s by John Smeaton, and the North Harbour some 50 years afterwards by Thomas Telford. This tells you of the importance of Peterhead as a fishing port for whaling and herring in the nineteenth century, for whitefish in the twentieth century, and as a supply base for the North Sea oil industry today.

■ St Andrews, Fife

St Andrews is the seat of the Royal and Ancient Golf Club, the well-publicised 'Home of Golf' (see **Activities, Golf**, above); it's also a famous old university town, a resort thanks to its sandy beach and golf links, and a town with a strong history of pre-Reformation religious leadership in Scotland – witness the magnificent cathedral ruins and the tall tower of the twelfth-century St Rule's Church.

▶ **www.standrews.co.uk**

RESORTS

■ North Berwick, East Lothian

North Berwick is an active little resort, dominated by the volcanic plug of North Berwick Law, which rises 613 feet in a steep cone at the back of the town. The Law is crowned by an arch made of the jawbones of a whale. North Berwick is a great golfing resort, and it's also the home of the Scottish Seabird Centre and the port of embarkation for boat trips to Bass Rock, the Isle of May and the Firth of Forth islets of Craigleith, Lamb and Fidra.

▶ *Boat trips to the islands arranged through the Scottish Seabird Centre* ✆ *01620 890202*; **www.seabird.org**

Useful Websites

www.nts.org.uk
www.snh.org.uk
www.goodbeachguide.co.uk
www.rspb.org.uk/scotland
www.historic-scotland.gov.uk
www.nnr-scotland.org.uk
www.visitscotland.com
www.visithighlands.com
www.undiscoveredscotland.co.uk
www.bbc.co.uk/coast

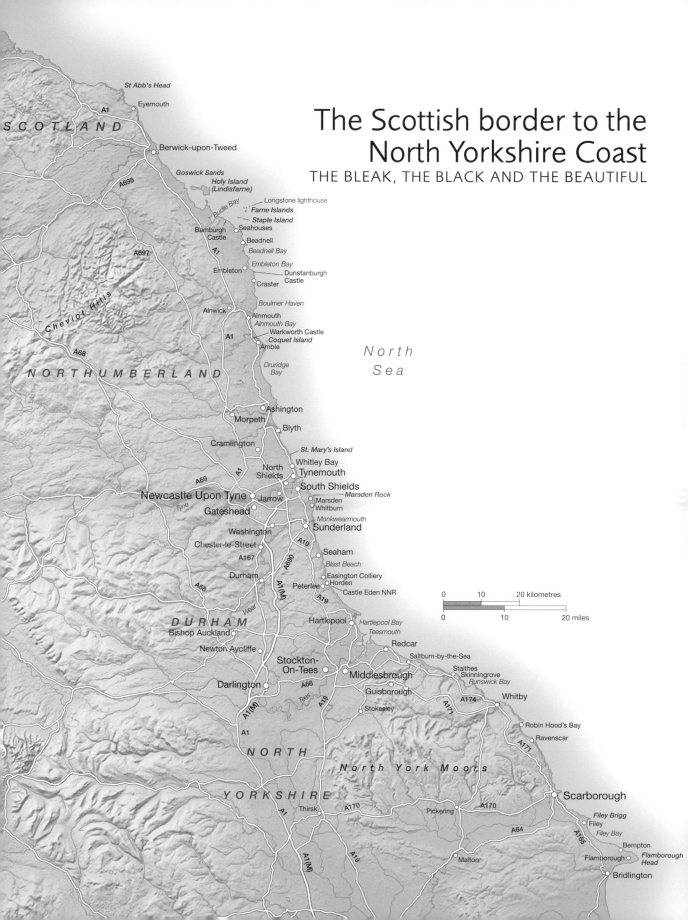

The Scottish border to the
North Yorkshire Coast
THE BLEAK, THE BLACK AND THE BEAUTIFUL

St Abb's Head

Eyemouth

SCOTLAND

A1

Berwick-upon-Tweed

Goswick Sands

A698

Holy Island
(Lindisfarne)

Budle Bay

Longstone lighthouse

Farne Islands

Staple Island

Bamburgh
Castle

Seahouses

Beadnell

Beadnell Bay

A697

A1

Embleton Bay

Embleton

Dunstanburgh
Castle

Craster

Cheviot Hills

Boulmer Haven

Alnwick

Alnmouth

Alnmouth Bay

A1

Warkworth Castle

Coquet Island

A68

Amble

NORTHUMBERLAND

Druridge
Bay

North
Sea

Ashington

Morpeth

Blyth

Cramlington

St. Mary's Island

Whitley Bay

North
Shields

Tynemouth

A1

A69

South Shields

Newcastle Upon Tyne

Jarrow

Marsden Rock

Marsden

Tyne

Whitburn

Gateshead

Monkwearmouth

Washington

Sunderland

Chester-le-Street

A19

A167

Seaham

A680

Blast Beach

Durham

Easington Colliery

A1(M)

Peterlee

Horden

A68

Castle Eden NNR

A19

Wear

DURHAM

Bishop Auckland

Hartlepool

Hartlepool Bay

Teesmouth

Newton Aycliffe

Redcar

Stockton-
On-Tees

Saltburn-by-the-Sea

Darlington

Middlesbrough

Staithes

Skinningrove

Runswick Bay

A66

A174

Whitby

A1(M)

Guisborough

Tees

A19

A171

A1

Stokesley

NORTH

North York Moors

Robin Hood's Bay

A171

Ravenscar

Scarborough

YORKSHIRE

Thirsk

A170

Pickering

A170

Filey Brigg

A1

Filey

A64

Filey Bay

A19

Bempton

A165

Malton

Flamborough

Flamborough
Head

Bridlington

0	10	20 kilometres
0	10	20 miles

ACTIVITIES

■ Birdwatching

Birdwatchers enjoy many a day travelling up and down the coast of north-east England. The Farne Islands are famous for their breeding seabirds in spring and summer, including guillemot, puffin and Arctic tern; Holy Island hosts curlew, turnstone, godwit and oystercatcher on its sand and mud flats; and Coquet Island holds sandwich, common and Arctic tern as well as the rare roseate tern and several other species including black-headed gull, puffin, eider and shelduck. Further south there are peregrines along the cliffs of the Durham and North Yorkshire coasts, and knot, ringed plover, redshank, shelduck and sandwich tern on the muds and foreshores of Teesmouth NNR.

■ Industrial archaeology

Lovers of industrial archaeology have plenty to study on this coast. Some examples are the eighteenth-century lime-kilns at Beadnell Harbour, the coal staithes or jetties at Amble, North Shields fish quay, terraced mining villages on the Durham coast, the great timber wharves at Hartlepool, the 'giant's geometry' of Teesside's chemical plants, the 'lost-and-forgotten' ironworking village of Skinningrove in the Cleveland cliffs, and the numerous alum and jet mines in the cliffs of North Yorkshire.

■ Sea-watching

The grey seals of the Farne Islands (see **Islands**, below) are a well-known attraction of the boat trips that run around the islands – you can see them hauled out on the rocks of Longstone and Staple Island, or putting their heads out of the water to return the curious stares of the boat passengers.

■ Walking

Beach walking on the firm, unfrequented sands of Northumberland is wonderful. There are two good coast paths further south – an 11-mile cliff path through the restored landscape of the Durham coast, and the 19-mile Saltburn-by-Sea to Whitby stage of the Cleveland Way National Trail.

▶ *Durham Coastal Trail: booklet guide from Peterlee TIC (0191 586 4450 or Durham TIC (0191 384 3720;* **www.durham.gov.uk**

▶ *Cleveland Way:* **www.clevelandway.gov.uk**

CASTLES

■ Bamburgh, Northumberland

Bamburgh Castle is spectacularly sited in the Northumbrian coast dunes on a high crag of the volcanic Whin Sill, looking out to the Farne Islands. The site has been fortified for at least 2000 years. The present stronghold contains a feasting hall with a magnificent timber roof within a grim Norman keep and medieval walls. The Armstrong family have held the castle since 1894 and have refurbished it and opened it to the public.

🚗 *Follow B1341 or B1342, off A1 between Alnwick and Berwick-on-Tweed (01668 214515;* **www.bamburghcastle.com**

■ Dunstanburgh, Northumberland

A fourteenth-century sea fortress standing in magnificent ruin on the coast, defended on two sides by cliffs and on the third by a man-made ditch dug through solid rock. You can climb to the top of the 80-foot-high gatehouse for a superb view over the coast and inland to the Cheviot Hills.

🚗 *1 mile on foot north of Craster (B1339) near Alnwick*

▶ *NT (managed by EH) (01665 576231*

■ Warkworth, Northumberland

The lofty thirteenth-century gatehouse and the great polygonal keep dominate this mighty grey stone fortress by the River Coquet. It was a Percy stronghold for 200 years until Tudor times; then the powerful Northumbrian family, often under a political cloud, fell into terminal royal disfavour, and Warkworth became a ruin.

🚗 *7 miles south of Alnwick on A1068 EH (01665 711423*

ISLANDS

■ Coquet Island, Northumberland

Cruising round little Coquet Island by boat from Amble, you'll be struck by two things: the 1841 lighthouse with its square tower, and the sheer number of seabirds (see **Activities, Birdwatching**, above).

🚢 *From Amble on A1068 (May–September), no landing (boatman (01665 711975), RSPB*

■ Farne Islands, Northumberland

The Farne Islands, outcrops of the dolerite mass of the

Whin Sill, rise out of the sea like surfacing sub-marines. Thronged with 100,000 seabirds and hundreds of seals, they are bare and windswept. On Inner Farne stands a pele tower and guest house, remnants of a monastery founded here by disciples of St Cuthbert, the original hermit of Inner Farne from 676 to 684. Longstone is the most seaward of the archipelago; it was from here on 7 September 1838 that Grace Darling and her father, keeper of the Longstone lighthouse, rowed through a storm to rescue nine of the 52 souls aboard the wrecked paddle-steamer *Forfarshire*.

🚢 *NT – from Seahouses (B1340). Cruise with option of landing on Inner Farne and Staple* ☎ *01665 721297;* **www.farne-islands.com**. *Cruise with option of landing on Inner Farne and Longstone* ☎ *01665 721210;* **www.lighthouse-visits.co.uk**

▸ *Grace Darling Museum in Bamburgh* ☎ *01668 214465*

■ Holy Island, Northumberland

Holy Island, sometimes called Lindisfarne, is connected to the mainland by a tidal causeway complete with refuge boxes. The island contains a village of 150 people, a great sandstone Norman monastery in poignant ruin, and the Tudor fortress of Lindisfarne Castle on a crag of the Whin Sill. In the Heritage Centre is a facsimile of the Lindisfarne Gospels (now in the British Library), regarded by many as the most beautiful book in the world, created by the Holy Island monks shortly after the death of their leader, St Cuthbert, in 687AD.

🚗 *Off A1, 5 miles south of Berwick-upon-Tweed. Accessible by tidal causeway; tide times from Lindisfarne Heritage Centre* ☎ *01289 389004 or Berwick-on-Tweed TIC* ☎ *01289 330733*

▸ **www.lindisfarne.org.uk**

■ St Mary's Island, Northumberland

A small tidal island off Whitley Bay (see **Resorts**, below), a great local favourite for a wander with its lighthouse (built in 1898), whose stairs you can climb for the view, and its rock pools and ponds that form a small nature reserve together with the shore.

▸ *Accessible from car park via causeway*

▸ *TIC* ☎ *0191 200 8650*

NATURAL WORLD

■ Beaches

Northumbrian beaches are lonely, windy and beautiful. The Marine Conservation Society names 12 in its Good Beach Guide; the coveted Blue Flag for cleanliness and conservation has been awarded to 10 of them. Further south the Durham beaches, once grossly polluted by mine spoil, are being cleaned up by man and the sea in partnership. To see how they used to look, visit Blast Beach (under Nose's Point just south of Dawdon), still half covered by a thick scab of 'minestone': colliery waste, grease and sludge several feet thick, like a poisonous miniature cliff.

■ Cliffs

The cliffs of the Durham coast account for half of Britain's magnesian limestone, an uncommon rock that supports such flowers as yellow rattle, eyebright, betony and many species of orchid. The sand, lime and mud rocks of the North Yorkshire cliffs are rich in minerals, and were mined in past times for the fossilized wood called jet and for alum used in the tanning industry.

■ Denes

The steep-sided, wooded clefts that cut down through the Durham cliffs to the sea are known locally as 'denes'. Casual waste-dumping grounds in the late twentieth century, they have been cleaned up and restored to their former glory as havens of wildlife for birds, wild flowers, trees and insects. Castle Eden Dene near Peterlee is a National Nature Reserve run by English Nature, while Warren House Gill and Foxholes Dene near Horden are now in the care of the National Trust.

■ Mud flats

Teesmouth National Nature Reserve consists of 880 acres of tidal mud flats, sand dunes and marshes, perfect for birds (see **Activities, Birdwatching**, above) and a breeding colony of common seals, the only one along this coast.

▸ *Footpaths to observation hides from Cowpen Marsh car park off A178, 4 miles south of Hartlepool*

▸ *EN*

■ Sea stacks

Marsden Rock in Marsden Bay, between Whitburn and South Shields, is a magnificent magnesian

The Scottish Border to the North Yorkshire Coast

THE BLEAK, THE BLACK AND THE BEAUTIFUL

limestone sea stack 100 feet high. A tall wave-cut arch pierced it until 1996 when the top of the arch collapsed.

■ Woodland
See **Denes**, above.

PLACES OF INTEREST

■ Beadnell, Northumberland
The great round-bodied lime kilns on Beadnell Harbour were built there around the turn of the nineteenth century to burn limestone for spreading as fertilizer on acid farmlands. They have also done duty as herring curing sheds.

🚗 *B1340 between Alnwick and Seahouses*

■ Berwick-upon-Tweed, Northumberland
In the medieval era, when rivalry for possession of the border lands was really hot between the English and the Scots, Berwick-upon-Tweed changed hands 13 times. These days it lies three miles into England, a handsome little walled town at the mouth of the River Tweed, connected to the south bank by three neighbouring bridges: a 15-arch sandstone road bridge of 1634, its 1928 concrete replacement, and Robert Stephenson's magnificent 28-arch Royal Border railway bridge of 1850.

▶ *TIC* 📞 *01289 330733*

■ Craster, Northumberland
It would be a pity to visit the picturesque harbour village of Craster and not buy a nice pair of Craster-smoked kippers – a local tradition that Robson's Smokehouse is upholding.

▶ *Robson's Smokehouse* 📞 *01665 576223;*
www.kipper.co.uk

■ Durham Heritage Coast
Before the last of the county's coastal coal pits closed in 1993, the cliffs and beaches of the Durham coast were so foul with colliery waste, coal dust, coal lumps and raw sewage that they seemed hopelessly blighted. But since then a vigorous clean-up campaign entitled 'Turning The Tide' has seen several locations along the coast designated SSSI (Site of Special Scientific Interest), and the area itself designated a Heritage Coast and an SAC (Special Area of Conservation).

▶ **www.durhamheritagecoast.org**

■ Easington Colliery, Co. Durham
Easington Colliery was purpose-built before the First World War to house workers in the newly opened mine. The pit, the last one to work the coastal seams, closed in 1993. With its red brick back-to-back terraces, steep streets, large chapels and miners' clubs, this is a typical County Durham pit village.

■ Hartlepool, Co. Durham
Old Hartlepool, the port that rose to prominence in medieval times, is clustered on the magnesian limestone headland called the Heugh. West Hartlepool, created around new docks in Victorian times, lies just down the coast and deals with North Sea oil and gas, timber and ship-breaking. Here, too, is Hartlepool Historic Quay, which recreates the early nineteenth-century days of sail.

▶ *Hartlepool Historic Quay, Maritime Avenue* 📞 *01429 860077*

▶ **www.destinationhartlepool.com**

■ Marsden Grotto, Co. Durham
Jack the Blaster, a limestone quarryman, started it all in 1782 when he blasted out a cave as a home. His cavern house soon became The Grotto pub – and you can still drink there today, riding down from the clifftop to the beach-level pub in a lift.

🚗 *Coast Road, Marsden, South Shields* 📞 *0191 455 6060*

■ Monkwearmouth, Wearside
The Saxon church of St Peter, Monkwearmouth, founded in 674 at the mouth of the River Wear, is all that remains of the monastery where the Venerable Bede (672–765) started his monastic life. Bede wrote hymns, religious contemplations, a life of St Cuthbert in prose and in verse, a history of the world, and his masterwork *Ecclesiastical History of the English People*. He must have been the most erudite and learned English writer of his day.

■ Seaham, Co. Durham
Seaham Hall, a fine big Georgian house, was the setting on 2 January 1815 for Lord Byron's ill-fated and unhappy marriage to local girl Annabella Milbanke, whom the rakish Byron thought was rich and might reform him: 'Rather dowdy-looking, though she has

excellent feet and ankles ... the lower part of her face is bad, the upper, expressive, but not handsome, yet she gains by inspection ... '

■ South Shields, Tyneside

Arbeia Fort guarded the entrance to the River Tyne in Roman times. Excavated and with some buildings reconstructed, Arbeia Roman Fort museum gives an authentic flavour of the power and precision of Roman rule in Britain.

▶ *Baring Street, South Shields* ✆ *0191 456 1369;* **www.twmuseums.org.uk/arbeia**

■ Staithes, North Yorkshire

Staithes is gorgeously situated in the North Yorkshire cliffs, the fishermen's houses piling steeply down to a harbour that shelters fishing boats with pointed bow and stern, called 'cobles' hereabouts. It was in Staithes in 1746 that a teenage James Cook, apprenticed to a shopkeeper, was accused of having been caught with his fingers in the till. Cook left Staithes for Whitby (see **Resorts**, below) and the sea apprenticeship that was to turn him towards becoming the greatest navigator and sea explorer of the age.

RESORTS

■ Saltburn-by-the-Sea, Cleveland

Saltburn's 600-foot-long pier is a reminder of the town's Victorian heyday as a seaside resort – as is the famous inclined cliff railway installed in the 1870s to take beach-goers to and from their hotels in the town above.

▶ *TIC* ✆ *01287 622422*

■ Whitby, North Yorkshire

Whitby is one of the most scenic and dramatic resorts in Britain, piled into a cleft in the North Yorkshire cliffs. Here James Cook lived for nine years in Grape Lane, learning about boats and navigation. Up on the south cliff stands squat St Mary's Church, with the grand ruins of Whitby Abbey behind. It was a scene used by Bram Stoker when he set tremendous, dramatic vampiric scenes in *Dracula* around the clifftops.

▶ *TIC* ✆ *01723 383637*

■ Whitley Bay, Northumberland

The Tynesiders' favourite seaside resort, with the old fishing town of Cullercoats on its south flank, Whitley Bay has a good sandy beach, plenty of amusement arcades and fish and chip shops, and the curiosity called the Spanish City, an amusement arcade dolled up to look like ... well, like a Spanish city.

▶ *TIC* ✆ *0191 200 8535*

Useful Websites

www.english-nature.org.uk
www.nationaltrust.org.uk
www.english-heritage.org.uk
www.goodbeachguide.co.uk
www.wildlifetrusts.org
www.rspb.org.uk
www.countryside.gov.uk
www.bbc.co.uk/coast

The Scottish Border to the
North Yorkshire Coast
THE BLEAK, THE BLACK AND THE BEAUTIFUL

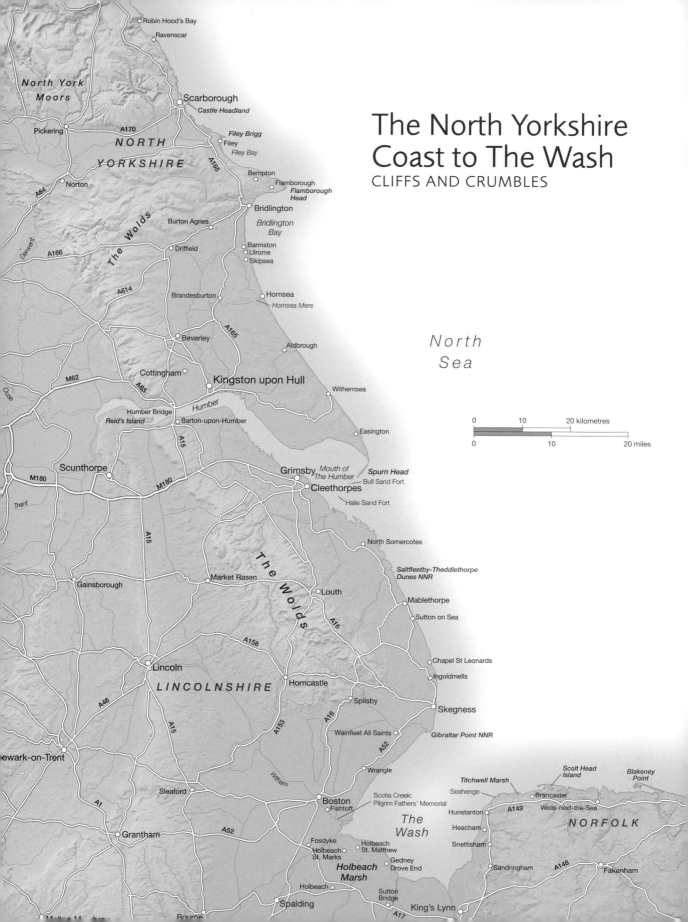

The North Yorkshire Coast to The Wash
CLIFFS AND CRUMBLES

North Sea

North York Moors

Robin Hood's Bay
Ravenscar

Scarborough
Castle Headland

Pickering

A170

NORTH YORKSHIRE

A64
Norton

A166

The Wolds

A614

A165

Beverley

M62

A63

Cottingham

Humber Bridge
Reid's Island

Barton-upon-Humber

A15

Scunthorpe

M180

M180

A15

Gainsborough

Market Rasen

The Wolds

Louth

A16

A158

Lincoln

LINCOLNSHIRE

Horncastle

A46

A153

A16

Spilsby

A15

ewark-on-Trent

A1

Sleaford

Grantham

A52

Witham

Boston
Fishtoft

Wrangle

Wainfleet All Saints

A52

Derwent

A185

Filey Brigg
Filey
Filey Bay

Bempton
Flamborough
Flamborough Head

Bridlington

Burton Agnes

Bridlington Bay

Driffield

Barmston
Ulrome
Skipsea

Brandesburton

Hornsea
Hornsea Mere

Aldbrough

Kingston upon Hull

Withernsea

Humber

Easington

Grimsby
Mouth of The Humber
Cleethorpes
Bull Sand Fort
Haile Sand Fort

Spurn Head

North Somercotes

Saltfleetby-Theddlethorpe Dunes NNR

Mablethorpe
Sutton on Sea

Chapel St Leonards
Ingoldmells

Skegness

Gibraltar Point NNR

The Wash

Scotia Creek:
Pilgrim Fathers' Memorial

Holbeach St Matthew

Fosdyke
Holbeach St Marks

Gedney Drove End

Holbeach Marsh

Holbeach

Sutton Bridge

Spalding

Bourne

Trent

Ouse

Titchwell Marsh
Seahenge

Brancaster

Scolt Head Island

Wells-next-the-Sea

Blakeney Point

Hunstanton

Heacham

Snettisham

Sandringham

A149

NORFOLK

A148

Fakenham

King's Lynn

A17

0   10   20 kilometres
0   10   20 miles

ACTIVITIES

■ Botany

The dunes, marshes and grasslands of this region are wonderful for wild flowers and plants of the coast. For example, Saltfleetby and Theddlethorpe Dunes National Nature Reserve in Lincolnshire produces orchids, cowslips, storksbill and cranesbill. At Gibraltar Point National Nature Reserve further down the coast, the dunes support pyramidal orchid, lady's bedstraw and cowslip; the flatter sandy areas are rich in forget-me-nots, dove's-foot cranesbill and saxifrages; and the plants of the freshwater marshes include yellow rattle and marsh orchid. Out on the salt marshes of the Humber Estuary and The Wash grow purple drifts of sea lavender, the pink nodding heads of thrift and the smooth, juicy nodules of glasswort or marsh samphire that gourmets enjoy as a pickled relish.

■ Birdwatching

For those interested in seabirds – kittiwake, fulmar, razorbill, guillemot, gulls and so on – the cliffs of North Yorkshire as far south as Filey Brigg and those at Flamborough Head in East Yorkshire are superb. Hornsea Mere supports wintering goldeneye, tufted duck and gadwall, and a late summer population of moulting little gull. The Humber Estuary is one of the top five British estuaries for overwintering birds. Clouds of migratory birds, including many rarities, drop in on the promontory spit of Spurn Head on the north bank of the Humber. In Lincolnshire little tern breed and thousands of waders roost at Gibraltar Point, while the scrub at Saltfleetby and Theddlethorpe Dunes National Nature Reserve is a breeding place for songbirds such as linnet, willow warbler and whitethroat. Hen harriers and owls prowl the marshes of The Wash, where the skies and vast mud flats are packed with overwintering geese and ducks.

■ Fossiling

Fossil fanciers will have a great time around the cliffs and beaches of the so-called 'Dinosaur Coast' of North Yorkshire – dinosaur footprints, belemnites and the teeth and bone fragments of marine fish-lizards from Whitby southwards; ferns and flowers in the Ravenscar area (now facilitated by the three-mile-long Ravenscar Trail; guide booklet from the Coastal Centre, Peakside, Ravenhall Road, Ravenscar ☎ 01723 870423); ammonites, bivalves and starfish around the cliffs of Scarborough's Castle Headland; ammonites between Filey and Bempton; and sea urchins, corals and sharks' teeth around the chalk cliffs of Bempton and Flamborough.

▶ www.dinocoast.org.uk

■ Walking

The final stage of the Cleveland Way National Trail runs for 33 miles along the North Yorkshire coast between Whitby and Filey. Beach walking is almost uninterrupted from Flamborough Head to Spurn Head, and from Mablethorpe to Skegness.

▶ www.clevelandway.gov.uk

NATURAL WORLD

■ Beaches

The sandy beaches of East Yorkshire stretch in a magnificent 40-mile run from Bridlington down to Spurn Head. It's the same story on the outward bulge of the Lincolnshire coast for 30 miles between the two National Nature Reserves of Saltfleetby and Theddlethorpe Dunes and Gibraltar Point.

■ Cliffs

The cliffs of this coast fall into two categories, north and south. The northern sector features the upstanding cliffs of North Yorkshire – sandstone around Whitby, limestone and mudstone near Robin Hood's Bay, sandstone and mudstone around Ravenscar, limestone from Scarborough south, and tall chalk cliffs at Bempton and Flamborough Head that rise to 440 feet and harbour England's biggest seabird colony. South of here the cliffs are low, black, bouldery clay, declining in height to the south and being rapidly cut into by the sea.

■ Dunes

Saltfleetby and Theddlethorpe Dunes National Nature Reserve (EN) features five miles of 700-year-old dunes rich in flowers and birds, and it's the same at Lincolnshire's other great dune reserve, Gibraltar Point (Lincolnshire Wildlife Trust).

■ **Estuaries**

Two of Britain's most important estuaries are features of this region – the five-mile-wide mouth of the River Humber marking the boundary between East Yorkshire and Lincolnshire, and the great square-sided estuary of The Wash, 15 miles across at its widest point, separating Lincolnshire and Norfolk. For seals, seabirds, wildfowl, coastal marshes, mud flats and wide open spaces under huge skies, the Humber Estuary and The Wash are supreme along the East Coast.

■ **Lakes**

Hornsea Mere lies just inland of Hornsea (see **Resorts**, below) on the East Yorkshire coast. At nearly two miles in length, this is Yorkshire's largest natural lake, with a big population of birds (see **Activities**, **Birdwatching**, above).

■ **Marshes**

The Wash contains the largest area of saltmarsh along this coast, the haunt of wading birds in the muddy creeks. Inland of the sea wall are freshwater marshes and vast areas of fertile farmland reclaimed from the sea – notably the great semi-circle of land north of the A17 between Sutton Bridge and Fosdyke.

■ **Promontories**

There are three 'hard' promontories on the Yorkshire coast – in North Yorkshire, Scarborough's Castle Headland is of hard limestone and Filey Brigg is a long headland of calcareous grits, while Flamborough Head in East Yorkshire is of hard chalk. The two 'soft' ones of the region are the sand and shingle spit of Spurn Head, and the dunes and marshes of Gibraltar Point in Lincolnshire.

PLACES OF INTEREST

■ **Boston, Lincolnshire**

St Botolph's enormously high tower, the famous Boston Stump, stands 272 feet tall over the Fen town where the religious dissenters who would later found the New World were jailed in 1607 for trying to escape the country (see **Scotia Creek**, below). Climb the Stump on a fine day and you'll get a wonderful view over the flat Fens as far as the towers of Lincoln Cathedral some 30 miles away.

▶ *TIC ☎ 01205 356656;* **www.bostonuk.com**

■ **Bull Sand Fort, Humber Estuary**

Bull Sand Fort, a squat toad of a First World War stronghold founded on a sandbank in the Humber Estuary, was built with its sister Haile Sand Fort in 1915 as a protection for shipping that gathered here to form convoys along the East Coast.

▶ **www.ecastles.co.uk/sands**

■ **Flamborough, East Yorkshire**

Surrounded on three sides by the cliffs of Flamborough Head, the village of Flamborough seems a remote place. You can get down to the shore under the cliffs at North Landing, and at South Landing, where the Flamborough lifeboat is housed. A few inshore fishermen of Flamborough still use cobles, wide-bodied boats with pointed bow and stern of a Norse design that has not changed in a thousand years.

🚗 *B1255 from Bridlington*

■ **Gedney Drove End, Lincolnshire**

Gedney Drove End is a remote village on the innermost shore of The Wash. Neighbouring Holbeach St Marks and Holbeach St Matthew are even more isolated, marooned among vast vegetable, corn and horticultural fields that have been reclaimed from the sea over the centuries. Only the high embankment of the sea wall separates the sea from the land that once formed its bed.

▶ *B1359 from Long Sutton*

■ **Grimsby, Lincolnshire**

Grimsby's famous trawler fleet is a shadow of its former self. But the town has played to its traditional strengths to boost its economy – it buys in fish and sells it through Grimsby fish market, and continues the business of processing and filleting fish as it has always done. Visitors can visit the fish market and a smokehouse, and learn of the fisherman's life and labour from retired trawlermen at the National Fishing Heritage Centre.

▶ *Alexandra Dock, Grimsby ☎ 01472 323345*

■ **King's Lynn, Norfolk**

King's Lynn lies on the east bank of the River Great Ouse on the Norfolk shore of The Wash. In medieval times the town was an important trade partner of the powerful German and Scandinavian ports of the Hanseatic League. There is a rich legacy of buildings from those prosperous days, notably the fine churches and two Guildhalls, and a Hanseatic warehouse near the quay – the only surviving example in Britain.

▶ *TIC (01553 763044*

■ Robin Hood's Bay, North Yorkshire

One of the most scenically charming coastal villages in Britain, Robin Hood's Bay fills a cleft in the cliffs south of Whitby. The red-roofed houses, standing at all angles to each other, seem to topple down to the sea. 'Bay Town' fishermen fish for crab, lobster and white fish caught on the long line. You don't have to stay here long to hear a smuggling story – Robin Hood's Bay is full of them.

🚗 *B1447, off A171 south of Whitby*

▶ *TIC (01723 383637*

■ Sandringham, Norfolk

Used by the Royal Family as a holiday refuge since it was built in 1870, Sandringham House has its main ground floor rooms and its museum of royal cars, photographs and gifts open to the public, along with extensive grounds.

▶ *(01553 612908;* **www.sandringhamestate.co.uk**

■ Scotia Creek, Fishtoft, Lincolnshire

Scotia Creek runs into The Haven, the mouth of the River Witham, three miles downriver of Boston. A memorial column marks the spot where William Brewster and his group of religious dissenters – known to us now as the Pilgrim Fathers – were arrested in 1607 as they tried to flee the country. The following year they did get away to the continent, and in 1620 crossed the Atlantic in the *Mayflower* to found a colony in the New World.

🚗 *2 miles south of Fishtoft, near Boston*

■ Snettisham, Norfolk

Tides play an important role at Snettisham Nature Reserve. At high water, spectacular numbers of dunlin and other wading birds retreat from the Wash mud flats to the strip of beach right in front of the RSPB hides. There are crowds of pinkfoot geese in winter, and of common tern in summer.

🚗 *Off A149 between Dersingham and Heacham*

▶ *RSPB (01485 542689*

▶ *Tide tables on RSPB website (see below); or phone RSPB Titchwell Marsh Visitor Centre (01485 210779*

■ Sutton Bridge, Lincolnshire

In early medieval times, before land reclamation, the River Nene reached the coastline of The Wash, where the town of Sutton Bridge now stands. This is where King John's treasure, including the crown jewels, is said to have been lost in 1216. The king's baggage carts were caught on the coast road by the incoming tide, and the treasure was swept away. Three miles north, on the east bank of the mouth of the Nene, stands East Lighthouse. A blue plaque records the residence of the naturalist and wildlife painter Peter Scott in the keeper's house from 1933 to 1939.

🚗 *Sutton Bridge: on A17, 8 miles west of King's Lynn*

🚗 *Lighthouse: from A17 bridge at Sutton Bridge, side road along east bank of River Nene*

RESORTS

■ Bridlington, East Yorkshire

Bridlington is a fine, traditional seaside resort on an excellent sandy beach, with all the resort trimmings from rock shops to donkey rides; it also offers Beside The Seaside, a hands-on museum of games, shows and vintage items celebrating the British seaside holiday.

▶ *TIC (01262-673474*

▶ *Beside The Seaside (01262-674308;*

www.bridlington.net/besidetheseaside

■ Filey, North Yorkshire

Filey offers seaside resort holidays, but it also has a fascinating history. In the nineteenth century the fishermen of the town were said to be the last heathens in Britain (see page 113). The Romans built a signal station on Carr Naze, the top of Filey Brigg (see **Natural World, Promontories**, above), and following identification of the Spittalls underwater structure on the south side of Filey Brigg as a Roman harbour, there seems every possibility that Filey was an important Roman port.

▶ **www.fileybrigg.com**

■ Hornsea, East Yorkshire

Hornsea has golden beaches and the lake of Hornsea Mere (see **Natural World, Lakes**, above). Hornsea Pottery has closed, but in its mid-twentieth-century heyday it produced beautiful designs that are now collectors' items.

▸ *TIC ☏ 01964 536404*

■ Ingoldmells, Lincolnshire

Billy Butlin opened his first holiday camp at Ingoldmells in 1936. There's still a thriving Butlin's resort here, incorporating the Fantasy Island theme park. This includes the Millennium Roller Coaster, a series of white-knuckle loops and twists 150 feet in the air at nearly 60 mph.

🚗 *A52, 3 miles north of Skegness*

■ Scarborough, North Yorkshire

North Yorkshire's best-known traditional resort, Scarborough still retains in its handsome old hotels, crescents and terraces an air of the elegant Georgian spa town – 'Britain's first seaside resort', as it styles itself. The two beaches and the two halves of the waterfront are neatly divided by Castle Headland with its twelfth-century castle keep behind long walls.

▸ *TIC ☏ 01723 383636*

■ Skegness, Lincolnshire

'Skeggy' is Lincolnshire's premier seaside resort, both made and mocked by the famous 1908 Great Northern Railway poster of the jolly fisherman skipping along a wind-blasted beach: 'Skegness Is SO Bracing!' The town offers a pier with lots of attractions, well-kept gardens, bowling alleys, amusement arcades – and a really fine sandy beach. It can be windy, mind.

▸ *TIC ☏ 01754 899887;* **www.skegness.net**

Useful Websites

www.english-nature.org.uk
www.nationaltrust.org.uk
www.english-heritage.org.uk
www.goodbeachguide.co.uk
www.wildlifetrusts.org
www.rspb.org.uk
www.countryside.gov.uk
www.bbc.co.uk/coast

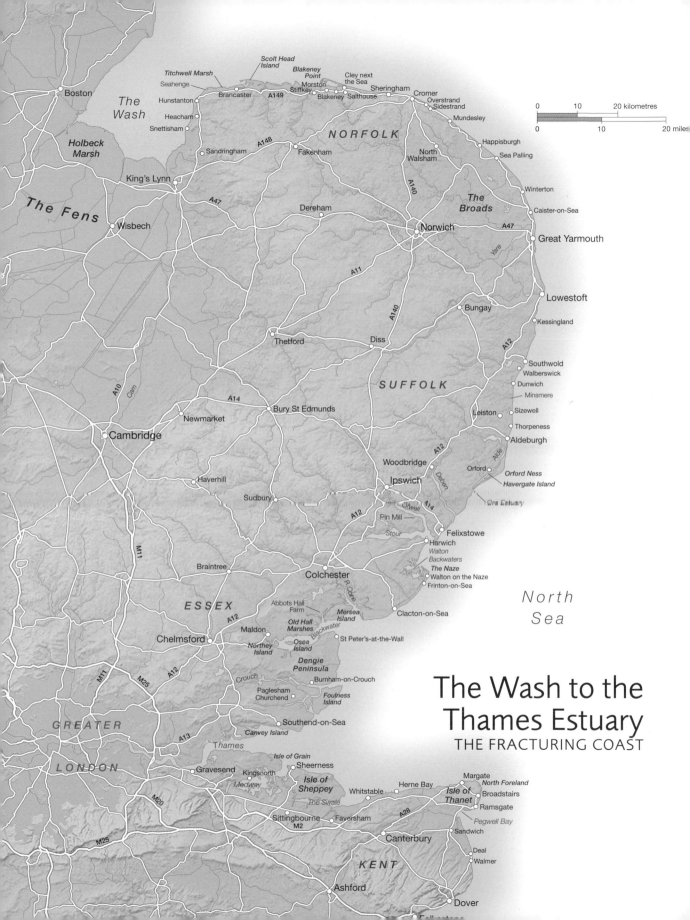

Boston

The
Wash

*Holbeck
Marsh*

The Fens

Wisbech

King's Lynn

Snettisham
Heacham
Hunstanton
Titchwell Marsh
Brancaster
*Scolt Head
Island*
*Blakeney
Point*
Morston
Stiffkey
Blakeney
Salthouse
Cley next
the Sea
Sheringham
Cromer
Overstrand
Sidestrand
Mundesley
Happisburgh
Sea Palling
Winterton
Caister-on-Sea

A149
Seahenge

Sandringham

A148

Fakenham

NORFOLK

Dereham

North
Walsham

A140

Norwich

*The
Broads*

A47

Great Yarmouth

Yare

A47

A11

A10

Cam

Thetford

Diss

A140

Bungay

Lowestoft

Kessingland

A12

Southwold
Walberswick
Dunwich
Minsmere

SUFFOLK

Sizewell

A14

Newmarket

Bury St Edmunds

Leiston

Thorpeness

Aldeburgh

Cambridge

A12

Haverhill

Woodbridge

Orford

Orford Ness
Havergate Island

Alde

Sudbury

A12

Ipswich

Deben

Ore Estuary

Pin Mill

Orwell

A14

M11

Stour

Felixstowe

Harwich
*Walton
Backwaters*
The Naze
Walton on the Naze
Frinton-on-Sea

Braintree

ESSEX

A12

Colchester

R. Colne

Maldon

Abbots Hall
Farm
*Old Hall
Marshes*
*Mersea
Island*

Clacton-on-Sea

North
Sea

Chelmsford

Blackwater

St Peter's-at-the-Wall

Osea Island

*Northey
Island*

*Dengie
Peninsula*

M11

M25

A12

Crouch

Burnham-on-Crouch

Paglesham
Churchend

*Foulness
Island*

GREATER

Southend-on-Sea

Canvey Island

A13

Thames

The Wash to the
Thames Estuary
THE FRACTURING COAST

LONDON

Gravesend

Kingsnorth

Isle of Grain
Sheerness

Medway

*Isle of
Sheppey*

The Swale

Whitstable

Herne Bay

Margate
North Foreland
Broadstairs

*Isle of
Thanet*

Ramsgate

Pegwell Bay

M20

Sittingbourne

Faversham

A28

Sandwich

M2

Canterbury

Deal
Walmer

M25

KENT

Ashford

Dover

0   10   20 kilometres
0   10   20 miles

ACTIVITIES

■ Birdwatching

Birdwatching is superb on the North Norfolk marshes, the Suffolk coastal heaths, and the tidal creeks and estuarine muds of the rivers Alde and Deben (Suffolk), Orwell and Stour (Suffolk/Essex border), Blackwater and Crouch and the Walton Backwaters (Essex), Thames (Essex/Kent), Medway and Swale (Kent).

▶ *Royal Society for the Protection of Birds (RSPB), The Lodge, Sandy, Bedfordshire SG19 2DL*

☏ *01767 680551;* **www.rspb.org.uk**

■ Sailing

Sheltered sailing can be enjoyed in Norfolk on the creeks around Brancaster and Blakeney, in Suffolk on the estuaries of Alde, Ore and Deben and from Pin Mill on the River Orwell, in Essex around Mersea Island and on the Blackwater and Crouch Estuaries, and in Kent on the Medway Estuary and in the Swale Channel between the Isle of Sheppey and the Kent shore.

■ Walking

Coastal footpaths include the Norfolk Coast Path from Hunstanton to Cromer (46 miles), the Suffolk Coast and Heaths Path (92 miles), sea wall paths along most of the Essex coast, and the Saxon Shore way from Gravesend to Hastings (163 miles).

▶ *Ramblers' Association, 2nd Floor, Camelford House, 87–90 Albert Embankment, London SE1 7TW*

☏ *020 7339 8595;* **www.ramblers.org.uk**

ISLANDS

■ Canvey Island, Essex

Its eastern half built up, its western half still green grazing marshes, its southern shore lined with oil and gas storage depots, Canvey Island lies behind stout sea walls on the Essex shore of the Thames.

🚗 *A130 from Basildon*

■ Foulness, Essex

Sited at the mouth of the Thames Estuary, Foulness is Essex's largest island, and has been perfectly preserved as a private enclave since 1915 by its owners, the Ministry of Defence.

🚗 *Normally no access*

▶ **www.stosyth.gov.uk/default.asp?calltype= foulnessmar01**

■ Havergate Island, Suffolk

In 1947 a few pairs of avocets – delicate blue-legged wading birds that had been extinct in Britain since the 1840s – reared chicks on this slip of a muddy islet in the Ore Estuary. They thrive here now, and have been adopted by the RSPB as its logo.

🚢 *Downriver from Orford Quay (OS ref TM390470); access by boat only*

▶ *RSPB* ☏ *01394 450732*

■ Mersea Island, Essex

Come to Mersea Island for sailing, for a nice long 12-mile walk round the perimeter, and to savour oysters at the Haward family's famed eatery, the Company Shed (☏ *01206 382700*).

🚗 *B1025 from Colchester*

■ Northey Island, Essex

Nowadays a wildlife reserve, but on 10 August 991 it was the setting for the Battle of Maldon. Saxon warlord Earl Byrhtnoth unwisely allowed a force of Danes, whom he had penned up on this tiny islet in the Blackwater Estuary, to come ashore. He and his followers were slaughtered.

🚗 *Near South House Farm, off B1018 near Maldon*

▶ *NT – visit by advance permit only* ☏ *01621 853142*

■ Osea, Essex

A privately owned island in the Blackwater Estuary just downriver of Maldon, one-mile-long Osea has an exotic history. In Edwardian times it was a sanatorium for well-heeled drunks and junkies, while during the First World War it served as a Motor Torpedo Boat base and had a population of some 2000.

🚗 *Normally no access*

■ Sheppey, Kent

The Isle of Sheppey boasts fine Georgian architecture in the old naval dockyard of Sheerness, splendid bird-watching on the Swale Channel and the southern marshes, and the early Norman Church of St Thomas at the south-western corner. In 1910 Muswell Manor, at the eastern end of Sheppey, was the headquarters of the infant Royal Flying Club. Such daring young men as Winston Churchill, Lord Brabazon and the

Hon. C S Rolls (later of Rolls-Royce fame) made
pioneering flights here.

🚗 *A249 from Sittingbourne*

▶ *TIC 📞 01795 668061*

NATURAL WORLD

■ Beaches

The wonderful beaches of the Norfolk coast form a
continuous strip of creamy-coloured sand running east
and south in a gentle curve from Sheringham to Great
Yarmouth, a distance of nearly 40 miles. A range of tall
sand dunes backs them for much of the way; between
Sea Palling and Winterton these are known as the
'Marram Hills' because of the spiky marram grass
that binds the sand together.

■ Cliffs

In North Norfolk, Hunstanton's cliffs are famous for
their red and white stripes, and Cromer's for their
crumbly consistency and frequent cliff falls. Down in
Essex the sand cliffs of The Naze near Walton yield
prehistoric sharks' teeth. The Thanet promontory of
Kent shows fine white chalk cliffs around Margate,
Broadstairs and Ramsgate.

■ Estuaries

Suffolk and Essex possess the best estuarine coastlines.
Suffolk has the Alde and Ore behind the shingle bar
of Orford Ness, the Deben running seaward from
Woodbridge and the navigable Orwell from Ipswich.
The Essex coast fractures into a maze of estuaries
and creeks, including the Colne from Colchester, the
Blackwater and Crouch framing the Dengie Peninsula,
and on the south the mighty Thames.

■ Heaths

The Suffolk coastal heaths, or 'Sanderlings', are a
precious habitat for rare birds such as woodlarks,
nightjars and stone curlews, which need this special-
ized habitat to nest and breed in. The Sanderlings
need careful management so that they don't revert
to scrub.

▶ **www.suffolkcoastandheaths.org**

■ Marshes

North Norfolk's saltmarshes have grown on rich silt
brought down from the farmlands and spread along

the coast by Norfolk's rivers. In summer they flush a
beautiful purple with sea lavender, while in winter they
are thronged with geese and waders feeding in the
creeks that intersect them.

NATURE RESERVES

■ Blakeney Point, Norfolk

Breeding tern, common and grey seals, rare
shingle plants.

▶ *Car parks at Blakeney Quay and Morston Quay*

▶ *NT 📞 01263 740480 (April–Sept); 📞 01263 740241
(October–March)*

■ Minsmere, Suffolk

One of the UK's best birdwatching sites, a 1500-acre
reserve of heaths, woodlands and lagoons, with a
wide variety of species including tern, breeding
bittern and marsh harrier, avocet, red-throated diver
and scoter.

🚗 *Signposted from Westleton on B1125*

▶ *RSPB 📞 01728 648701*

■ Old Hall Marshes, Essex (RSPB)

Moody, lonely marshland reserve with a big lagoon
that supports avocet and also ruff; huge numbers
of seabirds and wildfowl on the adjacent mudflats
in winter.

🚗 *North of Tollesbury, B1023*

▶ *RSPB 📞 01621 869015;*

www.southendrspb.co.uk/oldhall.htm

PLACES OF INTEREST

■ Abbots Hall Farm, Essex

With the low-lying Essex coast under threat from
rising sea levels, Essex Wildlife Trust has taken the
initiative by buying the 700-acre arable farm of
Abbotts Hall at Great Wigborough. Half will be
farmed in a wildlife-friendly way, while the sea
will be allowed to flood the other half to create
300 acres of new saltmarsh.

🚗 *Off B1026 at Great Wigborough, near Tollesbury*

▶ *Essex Wildlife Trust 📞 01621 862960*

■ Deal, Kent

It was on a beach between Deal and neighbouring
Walmer that the first Roman expedition to Britain,

The Wash to the Thames Estuary

THE FRACTURING COAST

commanded in person by Julius Caesar, landed on 25 August, 55 BC. The British charioteers gave the nervous Roman invasion force a hard time, but eventually they got ashore. Honours were even in the skirmishes that followed, and the Romans were glad to withdraw as soon as they could.

■ Dengie, Essex

A blunt-nosed arable peninsula sandwiched between the estuaries of Blackwater and Crouch, Dengie is superb for lonely walking and birdwatching. The Saxon chapel of St Peter's-at-the-Wall, Britain's oldest church still in use, stands on the sea wall at the north-east tip of Dengie.

■ Dunwich, Suffolk

Medieval Dunwich was one of East Anglia's most prosperous towns, with nine churches, two hospitals and two monasteries, a port, a market place and hundreds of fine houses. A tiny fragment of all this survives – the sea has taken the rest.

🚗 *Off B1125 near Westleton*

▶ *Dunwich Museum, St James Street, Dunwich*
☎ *01728-648796;* **www.aboutnorfolksuffolk.co.uk/ dunwichmuseum.htm**

■ Ebbsfleet, Kent

Sent from Rome by Pope Gregory the Great in the spring of 597 to convert the heathen British, St Augustine and 40 rather reluctant monks landed at Ebbsfleet in Pegwell Bay on the southern side of the Isle of Thanet.

■ Maldon, Essex

One of those places that aficionados like to keep for themselves as a nice secret, Maldon is a delightful old port on the River Blackwater. Its Hythe quay bustles with restored sailing barges, while round the corner the Maldon Crystal Salt company (**www.maldonsalt.co.uk**) makes salt from evaporated seawater.

▶ *TIC* ☎ *01621 856503*

■ Orford, Suffolk

A former port in a remote coastal location, Orford was cut off from the sea by the growth of the giant Orford Ness shingle spit. The Ness, MoD property for most of the twentieth century but now looked after by the National Trust, contains rare birds and plants, and a unique collection of Cold War buildings including atomic bomb testing laboratories.

🚢 *Orford Ness: access by boat only from Orford Quay at end of B1084*

▶ *NT* ☎ *01394 450900*

■ Sizewell, Suffolk

Twin nuclear power stations loom eerily above the shingly beach on this lonely stretch of the Suffolk coast – the stark grey cube of Sizewell A's Magnox gas-cooled reactor, and the white dome of Sizewell B's pressurized water reactor.

■ Thorpeness, Suffolk

Soaring 100 feet above the mock-Tudor holiday homes of this coastal hideaway is the House in the Clouds. It seems to be a weather-boarded Swiss cottage jammed on top of a five-storey house; but it's all a cunning sham. The cottage is a disguised water tank.

■ Walberswick, Suffolk

Each August the British Open Crabbing Championships (T-shirt slogan: 'I Caught Crabs At Walberswick') is held here. In bygone years Walberswick was famous for its large, half-ruined fifteenth-century Church of St Andrew, and its colony of landscape artists drawn to the subtle light of the Suffolk coast.

▶ **www.walberswick.ws**

■ Whitstable, Kent

The most picturesque port on the North Kent coast, with a harbour full of fishing and coasting vessels and lined with fish and sail sheds. Whitstable's native oysters, long off the menu, are back on sale, and you can sample them at the town's July Oyster Festival.

▶ **www.whitstableoysterfestival.co.uk**

▶ *TIC* ☎ *01227 275482*

RESORTS

■ Aldeburgh, Suffolk

A fishing village beloved of discerning holidaymakers, where boats land their catch straight onto the pebbles. The Aldeburgh Fish & Chip Shop (226 High Street ☎ 01728 452250) may well be the best in Britain. One of Britain's greatest twentieth-century composers, Lowestoft-born Benjamin Britten (1913–1976) lived at

Aldeburgh on the Suffolk coast from 1947 until his death in 1976. He is buried in the churchyard there.

▶ *TIC* (*01728 453637*

■ Clacton-on-Sea, Frinton-on-Sea and Walton-on-the-Naze, Essex

Essex's neighbouring 'Heavenly Trio': Clacton-on-Sea, the epitome of a brash, bouncy day-tripper's paradise; Frinton, a byword for genteel exclusivity; and Walton, the old-fashioned family resort.

▶ *TIC* (*01255 423400*

■ Cromer, Norfolk

A first-class example of a British seaside resort: small, friendly, family-orientated, with a fine sandy beach. Cromer has one of the country's last surviving 'end-of-the-pier' shows. Henry Blogg (1876–1954), an exceptionally brave and skilful saver of lives, served with the Cromer lifeboat for 53 years, 38 of them as Coxswain. In addition to a George Cross (the civilian VC) and a BEM, he was awarded three Gold Medals and four Silver Medals of the Royal National Lifeboat Institution – an unparalleled accolade. London journalist Clement Scott (1841–1904) came to North Norfolk in 1883 to write romantically for the *Daily Telegraph* of the rustic scene around Overstrand and Sidestrand on the cliffs east of Cromer. He called the area 'Poppyland', and created a huge late-Victorian tourist industry in these two tiny farming villages.

▶ *TIC* (*01263 512497*

■ Margate, Broadstairs and Ramsgate, Isle of Thanet, Kent

See **Clacton, Frinton, Walton**, above – these three neighbouring resorts reflect just the same values, and bear the same relationship to each other.

▶ *TIC* (*01843 583333*

■ Southwold, Suffolk

Solid, easy on the eye, with no hint of flash or brash, Southwold's holiday trade is founded on devotees who came as children and return with their own children, year after year. This is the East Coast's premier middle-class resort. The crime writer P D James, creator of fictional detective Adam Dalgliesh, sets many of her thrillers in Suffolk – two of the best-known being *Devices and Desires* (1991) and

Unnatural Causes (1993). She writes her books in a beach hut at Southwold, where she lives.

▶ *TIC* (*01502 724729*

Useful Websites

www.rspb.org.uk
www.bbc.co.uk/coast

Index

REFERENCES TO THE GAZETTEER SECTION ARE IN **BOLD**
PICTURE REFERENCES ARE IN *ITALICS*

Acknowledgements

Author acknowledgements: I would like to thank those who work for, or belong to, the Royal Society for the Protection of Birds, English Nature, Scottish Natural Heritage, Environment and Heritage Service for Northern Ireland, English Heritage, CADW, Historic Scotland, the National Trust and the Wildlife Trusts; and also to commend all the boatmen and beach cleaners, poets and painters, fishers and fiddlers, outgoers and incomers, birders, botanists, surfers, ramblers and motley crews of volunteers who together celebrate and safeguard our wonderful, irreplaceable coast.

studio cactus would like to thank Jason Hawkes (www.jasonhawkes.com) for the use of his photographs.

Maps by Martin Darlison at Encompass Graphics.

Photography credits p.2, p.4, p.6 Jason Hawkes Aerial Photography; p.8 © Andrew Parker/Alamy; p.9 Jason Hawkes Aerial Photography; p.10 © Denny Rowland/Alamy; p.11, p.12 Jason Hawkes Aerial Photography; p.13 © Jim Tampin/Alamy; p.15 © Boating Images Photo Library/Alamy; p.16 © Robert Harding Picture Library Ltd/Alamy; p.17 © Peter Barritt/Alamy; p.18 (top) © one-image photography/Alamy; (bottom) Jason Hawkes Aerial Photography; p.19 © James Davis Photography/Alamy; p.20 Jason Hawkes Aerial Photography; p.21 © Richard Hancock/Alamy; p.22 © Apex News and Pictures Agency/Alamy; p.24 © Jon Arnold Images/Alamy; p.25 © Eye Ubiquitous/Alamy; p.26 © Derek Stone/Alamy; p.28 © Jeff Morgan/Alamy; p.29 © Kevin Allen/Alamy; p.30 © Graham Bell/Alamy; p.31 © Jeremy Inglis/Alamy; p.32 © Robert Slade/Alamy; p.33 © Robert Slade/Alamy; p.34 (top) © Blue Eyes Photography Ltd/Alamy; (bottom) © Adrian Hawke/Alamy; p.36 © Peter Barritt/Alamy; p.37 © The Photolibrary Wales/Alamy; p.39 © The Photolibrary Wales/Alamy; p.40 © Chris Warren/Alamy; p.41 © Peter Packer/Alamy; p.42 © The Photolibrary Wales/Alamy; p.44 Jason Hawkes Aerial Photography; p.45 (top) © Ian Thraves/Alamy; (bottom) © The Photolibrary Wales/Alamy; p.46 © Blue Eyes Photography/Alamy; p.47 © Alan King/Alamy; p.49 © nikreates 2/Alamy; p.50 © The National Trust Photolibrary/Alamy; p.51 © Robert Harding Picture Library Ltd/Alamy; p.52 © Scenics and Science/Alamy; p.53 © worldthroughthelens/Alamy; p.54 © worldthroughthelens/Alamy; p.55 © Leslie Garland Picture Library/Alamy; p.56 © John La Gette/Alamy; p.57 © David Crausby/Alamy; p.59 © David Nixon/Alamy; p.60 © scenicireland.com/Christopher Hill Photographic/Alamy; p.61 © Shout/Alamy; p.63 © scenicireland.com/Christopher Hill Photographic/Alamy; p.64 © David Noton/Alamy; p.65 © scenicireland.com/Christopher Hill Photographic/Alamy; p.66 © Expuesto – Nicolas Randall/Alamy; p.67 © Jan Baks/Alamy; p.69 (top) © Chris Gomersall/Alamy; (bottom) © David Gowans/Alamy; p.70 (top) © Alan King/Alamy; (bottom) © Ronald Weir/Alamy; p.71 © Tom Kidd/Alamy; p.72 © nagelestock.com/Alamy; p.73 © South West Images Scotland/Alamy; p.75 (top) © Worldwide Picture Library/Alamy; (bottom) © Duncan Hale-Sutton/Alamy; p.77 © Niall McDiarmid/Alamy; p.78 © Doug Houghton/Alamy; p.79 © Andrew Bell/Alamy; p.80 © Travel-Shots/Alamy; p.81 © Jesus Rodriguez/Alamy; p.83 © Jim Henderson/Alamy; p.84 © AA World Travel Library/Alamy; p.85 © Doug Houghton/Alamy; p.86 © Navin Mistry/Alamy; p.87 (top) © David Lyons/Alamy; (bottom) © geogphotos/Alamy; p.88 (top) © Doug Houghton/Alamy; (bottom) © Worldwide Picture Library/Alamy; p.89 © Rolf Richardson/Alamy; p.90 © Doug Houghton/Alamy; p.91 © David Gowans/Alamy; p.92 © David Gowans/Alamy; p.93 © Worldwide Picture Library/Alamy; p.95 © Jon Arnold Images/Alamy; p.96 © Ronald Weir/Alamy; p.97 Jason Hawkes Aerial Photography; p.98 (both) © Leslie Garland Picture Library/Alamy; p.99 © Leslie Garland Picture Library/Alamy; p.100 © David Cattanack/Alamy; p.101 © The National Trust Photolibrary/Alamy; p.102 © Glyn Thomas/Alamy; p.103 © Brand X Pictures/Alamy; p.104 Jason Hawkes Aerial Photography; p.106 © Robert Harding Picture Library Ltd/Alamy; p.107 © Barry Wakelin/Alamy; p.108 © Darryl Gill/Alamy; p.109 © BL Images Ltd/Alamy; p.110 © The National Trust Photolibrary/Alamy; p.111 (top) © geogphotos/Alamy; (bottom) © worldthroughthelens/Alamy; p.112 © Worldwide Picture Library/Alamy; p.113 © Mike Kipling/Alamy; p.114 Jason Hawkes Aerial Photography; p.116 © Worldwide Picture Library/Alamy; p.118 © Roger Tidman/Corbis; p.119 © Julie Mowbray/Alamy; p.120 © David Moore/Alamy; p.121 © Les Polders/Alamy; p.122 © geogphotos/Alamy; p.123 (top) © Rod Edwards/Alamy; (bottom) © Neil Holmes/Alamy; p.125 © David Tipling/Alamy; p.126 © Geoff du Feu/Alamy; p.127 © Tony Lilley/Alamy.

This book is published to accompany the television series entitled **COAST**, first broadcast on BBC2 in 2005.

Executive Producer Gary Hunter
Series Producer Gill Tierney

Published by BBC Books, BBC Worldwide Limited, Woodlands, 80 Wood Lane, London W12 0TT

First published 2005
Reprinted 2005 (nine times)

Text © BBC Worldwide Limited 2005
The moral right of the author has been asserted.

ISBN 0 563 52279 8

Commissioning Editors Stuart Cooper and Shirley Patton
Project Editor Sarah Reece
Production Controller Alix McCulloch

Colour origination and printing by Butler & Tanner Ltd, Frome, England

For more information about this and other BBC books, please visit our website on www.bbcshop.com or telephone 08700 777 001.

Produced for BBC Books by

studio cactus ©

13 SOUTHGATE STREET WINCHESTER HAMPSHIRE SO23 9DZ
WWW.STUDIOCACTUS.CO.UK   TEL: 01962 878600

Design and Picture Research Sharon Cluett
Editor Clare Wallis
Proofreader Aaron Brown
Indexer Lynda Swindells